What People Are Saying About *The QB Mentor*

The QB Mentor is an inspirational story that artfully mixes elements of fatherhood, coaching, and faith. Readers from all walks of life, not just football fans, will enjoy getting to know Coach Wilson, Scott, and Shawn Stankavage and will be uplifted by how they deal with the challenges life presents.

—DARRIN D. GRAY, ALL PRO DAD, NATIONAL PARTNERSHIP DIRECTOR; AUTHOR, *THE JERSEY EFFECT: BEYOND THE WORLD CHAMPIONSHIP*

Truth comes through in a lot of different ways. I find that the two most powerful fountains of truth are the Good Book and the Book of Life. Scott gifts the reader by sharing his story—as an athlete, a father, and a man—and it is a story that shows us lessons that will drive you to seek things from life that are bigger and better than the humdrum of the everyday. Scott's life, and ours, is a classroom where strength in weakness, trust in unseen promises, perseverance, courage, and an eternal gaze are the greatest course offerings for the greatest of purposes!

—JAY THOMAS, LEAD PASTOR, CHAPEL HILL BIBLE CHURCH

You don't have to be the father of a college quarterback to appreciate *The QB Mentor*. It has something for everyone, especially those seeking to live life without regrets. Read it and be blessed!

—BRETT RUDOLPH, FORMER ALL-ACC LINEBACKER, UNIVERSITY OF NORTH CAROLINA

I couldn't put *The QB Mentor* down. A must read for coaches and parents at every level. The wisdom of Coach Wilson can apply to all walks of life and all occupations. Coach Wilson represents the best of all coaches everywhere. I wish every player and every father had a mentor like Coach.

—MATT DOHERTY, FORMER NATIONAL COACH OF THE YEAR, MEN'S BASKETBALL (NOTRE DAME); FORMER NORTH CAROLINA HEAD COACH; NCAA CHAMPION AS PLAYER (NORTH CAROLINA, 1982)

This book is the wonderful story of Steve and Scott coming together to tutor and father a young quarterback who faced adversity and challenges on the path to his dreams.

—DAN REEVES, SUPER BOWL HEAD COACH, FORMER HEAD COACH DENVER BRONCOS, NEW YORK GIANTS, ATLANTA FALCONS (FROM A WORD FROM DAN REEVES, INSIDE)

The QB Mentor was like Madden meets *Tuesdays with Morrie*. A truly inspiring book of courage, perseverance, and never-say-die attitude that will uplift everyone who reads it.

—ANTHONY DILWEG, FOOTBALL DAD; FORMER ACC PLAYER OF THE YEAR (QUARTERBACK, DUKE UNIVERSITY); FORMER QUARTERBACK, GREEN BAY PACKERS

The QB Mentor absolutely nails it from the perspective of a father wanting to set the table for his son, as well as a man battling a cancer diagnosis. I felt like Scott was writing about me and my family in so many ways.

—CHRIS WERNESS, CANCER SURVIVOR, FATHER OF A 10TH-GRADE HIGH SCHOOL QUARTERBACK, FOOTBALL DAD, CHIROPRACTIC PHYSICIAN

The QB Mentor was exactly what I was looking for to help my son and me in navigating his high school career—and the dreams he has set for himself.

—GEORGE MILLER, FATHER OF A HIGH SCHOOL QUARTERBACK, ATTORNEY

I have never read a better description of what it's like for a high school athlete chasing his dreams while facing such big obstacles in life. *The QB Mentor* was encouraging, inspiring, and left me and my son committed to overcoming any obstacle we might face in our lives.

—DAN BURMEISTER, FOOTBALL DAD, FORMER COLLEGE AND NFL PLAYER, FATHER OF AN 11TH-GRADE NATIONALLY RECRUITED QUARTERBACK

I was inspired by this story of hope, commitment, and most importantly, values-based leadership in a world that's becoming more complex every day. *The QB Mentor* goes beyond football to impart important life lessons for youth and adults alike. It's a must read: Coach and Scott have never been more on top of their games.

—LEIGH ANN SIMMONS, PH.D., ASSOCIATE PROFESSOR, DUKE UNIVERSITY SCHOOL OF NURSING; SPORTS MOM, AVID COLLEGE FOOTBALL FAN

Scott does a terrific job describing the recruiting process for so many kids today, and how important it is to have someone help you through everything that takes place.

—TONY CREECY, COACH, SOUTHERN DURHAM HIGH SCHOOL (STATE CHAMPS); COACHED SHAWN STANKAVAGE TWO YEARS IN POP WARNER; SON, SCHOLARSHIP PLAYER AT NORTH CAROLINA STATE

A phenomenal book that uniquely weaves the narratives of life, family, and football together with the message of faith and the "overcoming" power we can all achieve. *The QB Mentor* captivates your attention from the beginning. This incredible journey challenges dads to be better fathers, friends, and faith-walkers. This book has more than just a ton of football knowledge, which it does have! Its pages also pour out life application and faith principles. You will be inspired to live life with renewed faith and passion. A must read for those in all walks of life.

—BRIAN DULEY, LEAD PASTOR, NIKAO CHURCH, CHARLOTTE, NC

Scott Stankavage beautifully illustrates the relationship between lessons learned on the field and their impact in life off the field. His devotion to faith, family, and football is inspirational. You don't have to understand the game to appreciate the extraordinary dynamic between father, son, and coach chronicled in this coming-of-age story.

—LAURA FOSTER, LICENSED CLINICAL COUNSELOR, CHICAGO

The QB Mentor

Words of Wisdom from
an NFL Veteran for an
Injured Quarterback That Can
Improve Your Life and Career

Scott Stankavage

With Robert Irvin

Carpenter's Son Publishing

The QB Mentor

Published by Clovercroft Publishing, Franklin, Tennessee.

Cover Design by Adept Content Solutions

Interior Design by Suzanne Lawing

Edited by Robert Irvin

Printed in the United States of America

978-1-942557-10-4

To learn more from Scott and Coach Wilson,
visit TheQBMentorBook.com or ScottStankavage.com.

Contents

Acknowledgments, Dedication

In all things, may God receive the glory. This book is no different. My wife, Kate, deserves a huge thank you for her support as we journey together in this life with three older children and our three younger kiddos. She is the one who afforded my fatherhood so many hours of time to be with Shawn and Coach. My oldest daughters, Sarah and Shelby, have been so supportive in my battle with cancer, and my brother Bruce has lived each chapter as it has unfolded in our lives. I must also acknowledge my friend and Christian author, Michael Thompson, for his encouragement and modeling of how to bring a book to life. And finally, many thanks to Robert Irvin, for his diligent work in bringing order to our story.

* * * * *

I dedicate this book to all of us who were never really anointed as "the guy" in our sports or our lives, but through perseverance, hard work, and faith were able to accomplish our dreams and goals even in the face of significant challenge. It's for the dreamers who are filled with passion, faith, hope, and love, who, despite a myriad of twists and turns, continue to get up every day and do their best.

Foreword

Pep Hamilton, Former offensive coordinator
Stanford University Cardinal,
NFL Indianapolis Colts

Coach Steve Wilson recruited me to play quarterback at Howard University in 1992. The combination of academics and football attracted me to a decision that would shape the rest of my life. Coach would always preach, "Colleges don't make people, people make people."

Coach Wilson has been a father figure to me and many other former players for more than two decades. I have adopted many of his philosophies as a coach, teacher, and father. Though I have been trained and taught by some of the brightest minds in the football industry, Coach Steve Wilson stands alone for his impact on me.

Coach Wilson has perhaps the most unique background and collection of football experiences of anyone who has walked before him. After a ten-year NFL playing career, and with no coaching experience, "Coach" became the head coach at our alma mater. In only four years he was national Coach of the Year and Howard was an 11-0 national champion. During his head coaching career he was his own offensive coordinator, his own defensive coordinator, and eventually coached his own quarterbacks.

Coach Wilson's offensive prowess came from his experiences as an NFL cornerback defending the game's greatest quarterbacks and receivers. He learned defense from gurus like Denver Broncos defensive coordinator Joe Collier, Seattle Seahawks head coach Pete Carroll, and Cincinnati Bengals head coach Marvin Lewis. He combined the mentoring of such accomplished coaches with the influence of his father, NFL All-Pro running back "Touchdown" Tommy Wilson. Coach Wilson developed a unique and powerful coaching and teaching style that would affect hundreds of men. All of this experience gave Coach Wilson a perspective on football, and particularly coaching and teaching quarterbacks, that I have never seen duplicated in its depth, perspective, and success.

Several of Coach Wilson's Howard players went on to play or coach professionally. Jay Walker and Ted White were Howard All-American quarterbacks who played in the NFL. I've been an NFL and Stanford University offensive coordinator, and Roy Anderson and Jimmy Johnson work with NFL teams.

Howard University players are coaching at all levels across the country, from the NFL through college and high school. Many others enjoy successful professional careers as family men and outstanding citizens in all walks in life.

Coach Wilson mentored all of us, pushing us to learn the entire science of football, both sides of the ball, and every nuance and rule that applied to any position. In doing so he prepared us for successes beyond our wildest dreams. It was a form of empowerment that made him so special.

Reading *The QB Mentor* brings back many precious memories of all the stories, anecdotes, and life lessons that Coach Wilson has dispersed through the years. This is the inspiring story of Coach Wilson's journey with Scott Stankavage, a former Denver Broncos teammate, and Scott's son Shawn, an under-recruited high school quarterback. The time these three men spent together is a great read not only for football enthusiasts, but also for mothers and fathers who enjoy the story of a wise sage mentoring the next generation of young men.

Proudly, I was one of Coach's earliest protégés. I am pleased that his knowledge, love of the game, and fatherly instincts continued both on and off the field. Our coaching family tree is pleased to welcome Coach's latest protégé, Shawn Stankavage, and his family. We look forward to the unfolding of the rest of their story.

—PEP HAMILTON
OCTOBER 2015

A Word from
Dan Reeves

Steve Wilson was one of the smartest players that I coached in the NFL. His work ethic, combined with being a student of the game, made him a valuable member of both our Cowboys and Broncos teams. Scott Stankavage, similarly, was a hardworking, tenacious student of the game. We signed Scott as a free agent after his successful college career at the University of North Carolina, and he made our Denver Broncos roster and was a valuable addition to our quarterback group with John Elway and Gary Kubiak.

This book is the wonderful story of Steve and Scott coming together to tutor and father a young quarterback who faced adversity and challenges on the path to his dreams. The QB Mentor reflects the important skill sets and qualities that both Steve and Scott have used in their lives, both on and off the football field.

—Dan Reeves
Former NFL head coach, Denver Broncos,
New York Giants, Atlanta Falcons

Prelude

Some stories are great because they are true, and others are great because they actually happened. This story is both.

I have the privilege to share with the world the wisdom, insight, experience, and friendship of Coach Steve Wilson through my son's journey of chasing his dream as a high school quarterback wanting to play at the college level. But my son and I aren't the only ones who have sat at the feet of Coach. Hundreds of men have been empowered in their athletic careers and throughout their lives by Steve's coaching and fathering, through his stories, his parables, his challenges, and his encouragement.

I have been extremely blessed that my path crossed with Coach 30 years ago, and again upon his retirement.

I hope you enjoy his intersection with your life as you read *The QB Mentor.*

"Son, in order to help you, I have to access your mind. But first, I have to touch your heart. I can't help you as a quarterback unless I help you as a man."

—COACH STEVE WILSON

ONE

A Chance Meeting

"If ever I can help, just give me a call"

Fall, Shawn's Junior Year

I was sitting at Champs Sports Bar and Grill at the mall on a Tuesday in October. I was seated with my back to the window, which was not unusual. Somewhere in my travels I developed the knack—or some might call it an idiosyncrasy—of always wanting to see an entire restaurant while I'm dining. It's nice to see who is walking in and out for lunch, and occasionally I'll spot a friend or colleague or client to whom I can wave and say hello.

Just as my iced tea was being delivered, I noticed a group of four men walking to a table on the other side of the restaurant. I did not recognize the first three, but the last man caught my eye. I thought, *I know him*, and immediately began running a mental scan of facial and body-type recognition from years of meeting people. We all do it, but my processing seems to take longer these days, and more often than it used to, I come up with a blank or a question mark.

How did I know this African-American man, in his fifties, wearing a baseball hat and golf shirt with shorts and sneakers?

He had a bit of a potbelly, but he was otherwise muscular in his shoulders and neck, indicating he was probably a former athlete. He turned his face toward my side of the restaurant, and instantly I recognized Coach Steve Wilson. I hadn't seen Steve in almost four years. We had last connected at the local high school, where I was helping to coach the quarterbacks for a new head coach. We had a brief exchange in that meeting four years earlier and reminisced a bit about our time as teammates on the NFL's Denver Broncos.

When I realized who it was, I burst out with a "Coach!" that carried across the restaurant. Steve heard that "Coach!" and knew it was directed toward him. He turned to see who had called out and saw me waving my arm.

Coach motioned to his group that he would be right with them and moved toward my seat. I stood up and extended my hand for a shake, which he accepted, but then he pulled me in for bit of a bear hug and embrace.

"So how are you, Coach? What's keeping you busy?" I asked.

"Just working with a couple of teams during the season, trying to help coaches keep their jobs and help players realize their dreams," he replied. "Same old, same old."

Then Coach continued. "I have been watching that quarterback son of yours on TV every Friday night. He is tearing it up, having a great year. I knew he was going to be good, but he is really special. He's going to need an agent before too long."

I smiled proudly and thought to myself, *Yep, that's my boy.* Shawn was having a great high school football season, leading the Cardinal Gibbons High School Crusaders to an undefeated start. He was drawing plenty of attention in the media.

"Thanks, Coach," I replied. "He's having a great year. We hope it continues and we hope that colleges will notice and offer him a scholarship."

Coach replied, "Oh, he will have his pick, don't you worry. Just tell him to keep focused on Friday nights and the playoffs, and let the rest take care of itself."

And then he added, "Hey, if ever I can help you or your boy

with anything, just give me a call."

I said I would.

At that point, there was no way to know just how much this chance encounter would change my son's life—and mine—forever.

TWO

Playoff Thrills—
A Magical Game

"I'm ready, Dad!"

November

It was a cool, crisp night in early November in Raleigh, North Carolina. Perfect football weather: clear and cold. Shawn's words to me from earlier in the evening echoed in my head: "I'm ready, Dad." *Lord, this is as good as it gets,* I said in a short prayer.

Gibbons' playoff opponent was Grey's Creek High School, from Fayetteville. Grey's Creek was a strong, fast team that had *three* college Division I-caliber players.

Gibbons had talent as well, at running back, tight end, wide receiver, and particularly at quarterback. Shawn Stankavage's junior year had been sterling; it was a breakthrough season. He accomplished more than he could have imagined. For his mom and me, to see his talent blossom on the football field was exciting as we considered the possibilities for recruiting and a college career that could lie ahead. At six-foot-two and 180 pounds, Shawn wasn't the type of physical specimen that made you look twice, but he was special because he was a playmaker. He had just been named unanimous conference player of the year with more than 3,000 yards of total offense and 33 touchdowns during the regular season.

I know the reality here: there are thousands of parents whose athletic dreams go unfulfilled and who, instead, try to live out their hoped-for athletic achievements through their kids. They push them onto baseball fields, football fields, basketball courts, soccer fields, and much more, ignoring the obvious signs of disinterest or subpar talent.

But these things were never the case with Shawn. His mother and I had our own athletic careers and scrapbooks of memories. We had more than our share of success: me as an All-State high school player followed by a successful college career as a quarterback at the University of North Carolina. I even enjoyed the proverbial "cup of coffee" for three seasons as a National Football League backup. Shawn's mom was a superb athlete who was a world-class swimmer and United States Olympian in 1980. Even though we had been divorced for almost 15 years, we both still wanted our son to have the best opportunities possible to play the game that he loved for as long as he was able. Shawn dreamed of being recognized as one of the top high school quarterbacks in the country, maybe competing in the prestigious Elite 11 quarterback event and ultimately having his pick of which college to attend to play football. Those were our dreams for him as well. And tonight would be the first step toward making those dreams a reality.

* * * * *

Gibbons received the opening kickoff, and the Crusaders' first play was a double pass for a 60-yard gain, to the Grey's Creek 20. Two plays later, out of a no-huddle offensive set, Shawn faked the run and lofted a perfect spiral to his receiver streaking into the end zone. Just the way you draw it up: less than a minute of play, and Gibbons led 7-0.

After a Grey's Creek punt, Shawn ran for 45 yards, down to the Grey's Creek 10. Continuing in the no-huddle, Shawn took the shotgun snap, looking into the middle of the field to freeze the free safety; he then looked left to the corner of the end zone. His wide receiver was covered, so Shawn made the next read and threw the ball short to the underneath man, who made the catch at the 7-yard line and raced into the end zone untouched. Whammo. 14-0 Gibbons.

For the rest of the half, the Gibbons offense was flawless. Although the Grey's Creek team was bigger and faster overall, Shawn's mastery of the no-huddle offense was rattling them. They hadn't seen this kind of precision, accuracy, and timing, and by halftime Shawn had accounted for six touchdowns—four passing and two rushing—and he had accumulated more than 450 yards of total offense. The score at halftime was a stunning 56-7. Shawn certainly had been ready.

But I thought to myself: *Gibbons isn't seven touchdowns better than Grey's Creek.*

* * * * *

Grey's Creek received the second half kickoff and scored on an impressive eight-play drive, making it 56-14. On the ensuing kickoff, the Gibbons returner dropped the ball and ran just five yards before the coverage team drilled him. The Grey's Creek sideline erupted. Momentum had flipped and Grey's Creek certainly looked like a different team than the one in the first half. This game was far from over. In order to regain momentum, Gibbons needed a couple of first downs. Grey's Creek stuffed the first two running plays, and on third down I was confident that Shawn would be passing—but I was wrong. A draw play was stopped for no gain. Now a punt on fourth down, and the Gibbons punter shanked it, the kick traveling just 12 yards downfield.

Grey's Creek scored on the very next play. It was now 56-21, with nine minutes left in the third quarter. Now Shawn would be tested—tested on his ability to step up and lead his team to take back control of a game it had dominated in the first half.

Gibbons made two quick first downs. I felt mild relief that we had halted the Grey's Creek momentum. On the next play, I reached for my binoculars to watch Shawn closely because, from time to time, I could catch the hand signals he would give his teammates, and I could predict the play Gibbons was going to run. (This is the reason I have always sat on the visitors' sideline, so I can read the signals.) I saw Shawn wave his right hand in the air in front of him like he was drawing on a piece of paper and then, with his left hand, pat himself on the chest. That was Gibbons' signal for a quarterback draw, a quick setup as if passing, and then a run, up the middle, by Shawn.

After that first step or two back, Shawn darted into the line of scrimmage. He picked up the first block and began to accelerate upfield. He cut left to avoid a linebacker diving at his legs. Once Shawn got past the initial wave of defense and was in the defensive second level, he began to set up the Grey's Creek safety, trying to fake him left and then cut back right for the chance to break away for what looked like it could be a 50-yard touchdown run.

Now standing in the bleachers, along with everyone else, I put the binoculars down in anticipation, as Shawn had only one player to beat—and this would be a pretty impressive addition to his highlight reel for college coaches.

Here we go, Son, I thought, smiling to myself.

'Get Up, Son'

Suddenly, Shawn was on the ground. I couldn't see how it happened, and there was a collective groan from the Gibbons sideline as Shawn hit the ground. Everyone sat down, except me.

As a parent, every time your son runs the football and is knocked to the ground, you keep your eyes on him until you see him get up. It didn't look like the Grey's Creek safety actually tackled him; it almost looked as if Shawn slipped or fell or something strange had happened. So I kept standing, curious, concerned.

Shawn stayed on the turf.

Get up, Son. You're OK. Get up.

Shawn tried, but he fell back down and put both his hands on his left knee. My heart sank; that was the last posture I wanted to see.

The play was obviously a long first down, and the normal mode of operation for this offense was to run to the line of scrimmage and snap the ball to keep the defense on its heels. But nobody was rushing to the ball. Shawn was down; Shawn was hurt.

The stadium went quiet.

One of Shawn's teammates bent down to help him up, but Shawn waved him away. The teammate motioned to the sidelines and the head coach and the trainer come jogging onto the turf.

The men around me put their hands on my back and patted my shoulder. "He's OK, pops." . . . "He's just catching his breath." I hoped so, but I also knew this wasn't his style. Shawn did at times play some possum in his career, but usually when he was tired. He never wanted the opponent to know it had hurt him, so he always tried to jump up, even on the hardest hits.

So when Shawn didn't get up this time, I was afraid something was really wrong.

After several minutes on the field, teammates helped Shawn to his feet. He tried to put weight on his left leg . . . The crowd applauded, both the home team and visitors, a sign of respect and sportsmanship from both schools.

Play resumed as Gibbons' backup quarterback took over. I looked through the binoculars at Shawn sitting on the bench with a crowd of players and trainers and coaches around him. He wasn't crying and didn't appear to be in any great pain. I was hoping it was just a sprain or hyperextension.

When Shawn heard the roar from the visitors' stands after another Grey's Creek touchdown, he got up from the bench and jogged down the sidelines by himself. I was watching through the binoculars, and I didn't see him wincing with any obvious signs of pain. *Surely he couldn't be running if the injury were serious, like a tear or something.* It was probably just a sprain, and perhaps he would still be able to play, I thought, hoped, and actually prayed.

But then I saw him slow his jog to a walk, and it took him nearly 20 yards to come to a complete stop. That wasn't normal. He turned around and jogged back toward the bench. His mom had come down from the stands and was now among the crowd on the sidelines.

Shawn couldn't stop his jog. Something wasn't right with his knee. He sat back down on the bench, and I lost sight of him with so many players around him.

I sat down too. But then my cell phone rang. It was his mom's number. When I answered, it was Shawn. "Dad, can you come down here?"

"Be right there," I said, ending the call.

The Longest Walk

I walked down the bleachers on the Grey's Creek side, onto the track, and walked around the north end zone to the home team's bench. It was a long walk around that track to see Shawn.

My mind raced. I was anxious, I was worried, I could see panic not far away, and I was concerned for my son's frame of mind. I never had a career-altering injury, and what if Shawn was facing that now? What impact would this moment have on his future, recruiting, college football scholarships, his basketball season?

I thought about what Shawn must be feeling, the thoughts in his head. Was he thinking the worst? Thoughts like, *Why me?* . . . *What about recruiting?* . . . *Lord, are you still with me?*

When I finally arrived on the sidelines, Shawn was the only one seated, so I sat down next to him. His uniform was wet with sweat and there was steam still coming off his head. His eye black was smeared on his face and his hair wet and disheveled. He looked at me and I looked at him. Neither of us knew what was wrong, and neither of us wanted to pretend to know. We just knew we had each other, no matter what. Sitting there next to Shawn, I kissed him on the side of his head and said, "I love you, dude."

"Love you too," he replied.

The team doctor came over to talk to me, Shawn, and his mom.

"It's definitely loose, looser than it should be. His ACL is probably torn, but possibly not, because some athletes have looser knees than others, and Shawn could be one of those kids with an unusually loose knee. The only way we can know is to do an MRI tomorrow. I don't think he should play any more tonight."

That was my opinion too, but I had not revealed it. I looked at Shawn and asked, "What do you think?"

"Dad, I want to play if I can," Shawn answered, calmly. "They need me. I don't want to lose this game."

I looked at him and said, somewhat sternly, "Son, you are done for tonight. Let's pray it's a sprain, get the MRI tomorrow, and we can make a plan from there. You have your basketball season and then the recruiting and summer camps. So let's focus on that, OK? That's what I think." Then I turned to Shawn's mom. "Mom, what do you think?"

She nodded in agreement. I could tell she was anxious and worried, hoping and praying that the injury wasn't a torn ligament. But there was nothing to be done for this night. Except ice and ibuprofen and keeping the leg elevated. We would get the MRI in the morning.

* * * * *

At the end of the night, as I got up from the bench beside Shawn, I glanced at the final scoreboard: Gibbons 56, Grey's Creek 52.

What a draining, exhausting game—in every way. Gibbons won and Shawn's statistics were 18 for 21 passing for 331 yards and four touchdowns, and he rushed for 104 yards on 12 carries and two touchdowns. Heck, of course I'm biased, but it was the finest performance by a high school quarterback I had ever witnessed. Four hundred and thirty-five yards of total offense and six touchdowns in just a bit more than one half of play is . . . well, astounding.

Shawn celebrated the bittersweet victory on crutches in the locker room with his teammates. Everyone wished him well. The coach announced that his injury was unknown, but that he was having an MRI in the morning, and we would know more at that time. He said everyone was hoping it was just a sprain so Gibbons could have its leader back for the next playoff game, a rematch against a powerful Hunt High School team that had knocked Gibbons out of last year's playoffs. This time the game would be at home for Gibbons, and the Crusaders would look to keep their undefeated season intact and keep streaking toward a state championship.

I offered to drive Shawn's car home that night, but he insisted he was able to drive. He actually hung out with the team after the game. *How much pain can he be in?* I thought, trying to put the best face on things. *Heck, he went out and got hot dogs. There's a chance that it's just a sprain.* And that was my prayer the rest of the night. *Lord, let it just be a sprain.*

I had been fortunate that the success of my athletic and business career afforded me the opportunity to rub shoulders and get to know doctors like the head of orthopedic surgery at Duke Medical Center. It was a privilege, and now this privilege extended to my son. As I drove home, I dialed the cell of Dr. Tee Moorman. Dr. Moorman is a former Duke offensive lineman who had followed his father's footsteps into medicine. Dr. Tee had done my shoulder surgery just one year earlier. I had the rotator cuff and the labrum repaired from years of wear and tear, throwing footballs, and lifting weights beyond what a normal shoulder is expected to endure.

I left a voice mail.

Dr. Tee called me back at 4 a.m. and left this message: "I have Shawn set up at Duke South Clinic for an MRI at 10 tomorrow morning. I will be able to read it around lunchtime, and I will call you as soon as I see the film. Keep the faith, my friend. Whatever needs to be done, he will be in good hands."

That was the message I needed to hear. Calm, experienced, and confident. It was the same demeanor I wanted to offer to my son.

* * * * *

Dr. Moorman called us on Saturday afternoon as we were watching college football on TV. He said he had reviewed the film. And then the truth came out: "Shawn has a classic ACL tear."

My heart sank. It was all I could do to not drop the phone and scream as loud as I could. But I needed to listen to the prognosis. "He tore the ligament right through. And as bad as that sounds, it's actually a good thing, because we can repair it with a tendon taken from the same leg and do what is called a reconstruction. The other good news is that he did no damage to the meniscus, and that is huge. We have gotten pretty good at ACL repairs, but the meniscus is a little trickier, and Shawn has no problem there. So I have scheduled Shawn for an 11 a.m. appointment to see me Monday morning. This injury can sometimes be treated without surgery, and we just focus on strengthening everything around the ligament—but that is not my recommendation. With a mobile young athlete and his entire future ahead of him, I will tell you that if it were my son, I would go in and do the reconstruction, and we can make that ligament strong as new. And with the rehab program we have developed, he will end up stronger in both his legs and knees than he was before the injury."

I kept my words to a minimum. "OK, doctor. Thanks for everything. We will see you Monday at 11."

The call ended; the world had changed for Shawn.

Basketball was over for his junior season. That alone was heavy. But the next issue became the football recruiting season of the following spring. The Nike camp and the combine and Shawn's hopes to participate in the Elite 11 competition. And then the college camps he hoped to attend in the spring, at Vanderbilt and the University of North Carolina and North Carolina State University and Stanford and Georgia and Tennessee. What about all of those dates?

These thoughts created a panic in me. I presume they did the same for Shawn. I wanted to, and needed to, address them out loud. And I needed to do it right then and there.

I looked at Shawn and said, "Hey. You know the Lord is in this, don't you? I don't understand it. I don't like it. I don't agree with it. But He hasn't abandoned you or your future or your career or your dreams. You got that?"

Shawn shook his head, slightly teary-eyed. I can't say if he cried because he was scared or because he no longer knew what his plan was for the future. This was a huge change of plans, a torn ACL in the middle of his junior year of high school. No other way to put it: this was devastating.

At the same time, Doctor Tee's words left plenty of hope. We could reconstruct it and rehab it and come out even better than before. *Could*. It *could* work out that way.

And in that moment I remembered something a friend once told me in high school: "Faith isn't faith until it's all you are left holding onto."

I hoped Shawn had a good grip on his faith. Time would tell.

THREE

Surgery and Recovery

*"Dad, will you tell Saban I will be
ready to go next season?"*

December

We met in person with Dr. Moorman on Monday.

It was a unanimous, no-brainer decision to have the surgery. Shawn's mom asked the doctor, "What would be the schedule for his recovery, and when could he return to competition like the college recruiting combines in football, and spring basketball camps?"

"That will depend on how hard he works in rehab," Dr. Moorman answered. "I don't like to give a schedule, but I can tell you that we will appoint David Roskin, one of the top PT [physical therapy] men I have ever worked with, to oversee Shawn's recovery. David is the best. Scott, you can attest to that from your work with him on your shoulder, correct?"

"Absolutely," I replied.

I pressed the doctor for a schedule, knowing that as an athlete, Shawn would want a target and a goal he could work toward.

"Look, why don't you go down and see if Roskin has a minute and introduce Shawn to him and ask him for a timetable. He will be the one responsible for it, so I am going to defer to him."

I had more. "How soon can we get Shawn in for surgery? The sooner we get it done, the sooner he can start to rehab and recover, right?"

Doctor Moorman said he would check the operating schedule next, and suggested we go visit Roskin. But before he left, the doctor reassured Shawn: "We look forward to getting you fixed up and back to playing at the high level you were at, if not even better, OK Shawn?" He gave Shawn a small pat. What a professional; what a relief to have this man on our team.

Shawn looked at me and said, "Let's do it."

The operation was set for November 14, a Wednesday. That is a good day. All through my playing career, from junior high school to the NFL, I was able to wear jersey number 14. I took that as a good sign.

Surgery . . . and Beyond

David Roskin saw me, Shawn, and his mom standing in the doorway of the physical therapy room, and said from across the room, "Hey, the greatest Tar Heel quarterback of all time, what's up?"

I smiled. That moniker probably wasn't true, but it made me feel good anyway.

David came over, extended his hand, and said, "How are you, my friend? You look great."

David always made you feel good when you saw him—both physically and mentally. He was a true healer.

I introduced him to Shawn's mom and then to Shawn, who was standing on his crutches. David asked what happened, and Shawn told him about the previous Friday night.

"Well, that's too bad," David began. "I hate to see your junior season end that way, but you are definitely in the right place. Dr. Tee will get you repaired, and we will take care of the rest down here. You will be in great hands."

I asked David for a typical ACL rehab schedule, and he hemmed and hawed like professionals always do, saying things like, "Well, everybody is different," and "Depends on how hard he works."

In the end, we left realizing that Shawn would be facing an intense six-month rehab before he was ready to be released to work out without restrictions. It would be at about the nine-month mark that Shawn could expect to compete without limitation. That would be mid-August, well into the preseason for his senior season of football. And the reality was that the ACL ligament and knee itself would not be fully recovered until about 12 months after surgery, but Shawn could expect to be recovered and playing at a high level before that.

We talked about Adrian Peterson's miraculous recovery, and then we compared it with Derek Rose and his ACL, which was talking longer to rehab. (Peterson is the Minnesota Vikings' All-Pro running back, who came back from an ACL tear in record, and remarkable, fashion; Rose the Chicago Bulls' first team All-NBA guard whose injury took longer to recover from.) The two athletes provided an illustration of why David did not want to give an exact timeline, but gave us ranges to use as guidelines instead.

Regardless of Shawn's timeline, we left knowing we would be in great hands throughout the process.

* * * * *

Shawn's anterior cruciate ligament reconstruction surgery was set for 7:30 a.m.

Shawn didn't seem too nervous as a series of nurses and anesthesiologists paraded through our curtained-off portion of the triage area. Dr. Moorman was the last person to visit. "Good morning, folks. Great day to fix an ACL!" We all smiled, and he asked Shawn how he was feeling. Shawn said great, adding "Ready to go!" Dr. Moorman explained that the procedure would take about two hours and that the plan was to harvest some of his patellar tendon and then string it through his left knee to reconstruct his ACL. He said the film didn't show any other damage, but he would be looking to confirm that, and if he saw anything that needed cleaned up, he would go ahead and do it while he was in there. We all agreed that was a good plan.

Then Dr. Moorman looked at me, and then Shawn's mom, and asked, "May I say a prayer over Shawn?" What a compassionate man. We both nodded yes, and Dr. Moorman reached out and we all held hands as he offered a simple prayer for healing and skill and a successful procedure on Shawn's knee so he could return to his athletic career. It was perfect. We all felt that we were in the best of hands.

The nurses soon wheeled Shawn's bed out of our waiting area. His mom and I kissed him on the head and wished him luck and told him we would see him on the other side.

It was a long two hours, but finally a nurse emerged. "Shawn is resting in recovery, and you can come back to wait for him to wake up," she said.

When we got there Shawn's knee was elevated and wrapped in an ice massage contraption that continuously circulated cold water around the joint. Shawn was still slightly sedated, but he recognized us as we came in his room.

"Hey, how do I look?" he asked, smiling.

"Great!" his mom and I both said, laughing.

"How did it go?" he asked, still a bit groggy.

We told him that Dr. Moorman visited with us and said it couldn't have gone better.

The next words out of Shawn's mouth were, "Good. Dad, will you tell Coach Saban [Nick, the head coach at Alabama] that I will be ready to go next season?"

I smiled and told him sure.

Shawn hadn't lost his sense of humor, nor had he lost his dream that he would one day play in the Southeastern Conference (SEC), either for Alabama or against them.

* * * * *

They moved Shawn to a room on a lower level, and his mom stayed with him all day. I left to go home. Around dinnertime my wife, Kate, and I packed up Shawn's 3-year-old brother, Leo, and Leo's twin sister, Ella, along with our youngest daughter, 1-year-old Jordan, and took them to see Shawn at the hospital. When we got there, the kids were climbing all over their big brother. We were all a bit nervous that they would jump on Shawn's knee, which was still elevated and attached to the ice massage machine.

Leo found Shawn's crutches and was busy for the entire twenty-minute visit climbing on them. The girls just sat on their big brother's lap, up in bed with him, smiling and loving on Shawn. It was a warm feeling for all of us, a nice emotion after a rough week.

Shawn said that his high school coach had been by to see him, which was a nice gesture. He had prayed with Shawn for healing and recovery, and told Shawn that he had ACL surgery his junior year in college and that coming back was hard work, but he expected Shawn to come back even stronger than before. Shawn was encouraged and appreciative of the visit, and so were we.

Shawn came home the next day. He wasn't too skilled with his crutches, but he managed. I gave him some lessons from what I could remember from my many times on crutches through my athletic career.

Shawn experienced some pain those first few days and nights. He wondered why, and I explained to him that they had drilled holes in his knee bones to insert a tendon, and then they had screwed the ends of the tendon into the top and bottom of his knee joint. "That leaves a mark," I explained with a smile, and he understood. He wasn't big on the pain meds; he felt they made him loopy and upset his stomach.

* * * * *

After three days of constant icing, the swelling had come down and Shawn was able to be on the sidelines, with crutches, to encourage his teammates in their next playoff game against Hunt. Despite a valiant effort, Gibbons lost and the Crusaders' season was over, and it felt like a premature end. Dreams came up short, potential unrealized. It was a tough week at school.

In physical therapy, David started each session with massage;

his goal was to soften the muscles around the joint and prepare them to start moving again. Even though it had only been a little more than a week since the surgery, the muscles had begun to shut down. David, and Shawn, needed to wake them back up. Immediately, David wanted to begin to force flexion into the knee joint; it would become stiff and rigid otherwise. Time was of the essence. David set an aggressive schedule for Shawn, which included stretching and wading in the pool in the second week, then walking without crutches thirty days out from surgery, leg presses with weights sixty days out, running in ninety days, agility drills after 120 days, going full speed in 150 days, and potentially playing basketball in 180 days, or six months.

That was amazing to me, to think that Shawn could rehab and recover from such a major surgery that quickly. David admitted it was aggressive, but he knew what Shawn's mind-set had been, and he also understood Shawn's urgency to get healthy so he could possibly pursue his basketball career and work out at college football combines.

* * * * *

Coach Wilson had been keeping tabs from afar on Shawn's injury and subsequent surgery. He called me around Christmas to say happy holidays and to check on Shawn and his progress. After some chitchat, Coach turned a bit more serious and said he had coached dozens of players who had dealt with torn ACLs, and he knew it was a long, difficult process, and there was work to be done—not only physically, but mentally and emotionally as well. As always, he offered his help if we needed him.

* * * * *

Physically, things progressed on schedule. I attended Shawn's first two sessions with David. His mother did also. Soon Shawn was going to PT two to three times a week, and Shawn's mother and I realized there was no need for us to be there. Shawn was in good hands, and if he was going to get healthy, there wasn't much we could do about it; he had to get there himself.

I signed Shawn and myself up for a membership at the local gym so we could also lift weights together twice a week. The truth of the matter was that Shawn had never really lifted weights for bulk or power, like football players do, in part because he was also a standout basketball player who had college scholarship interest from mid-major schools, and he had not yet totally committed himself to either sport. I knew, though, that to become qualified as a prospect as a major college quarterback, we had to change Shawn's physique.

Shawn went at it hard, and it was bonding time for my son and me. I probably loved it more than he did. But I also began to notice that after about the second month, I would get winded much more quickly than he did. I also didn't make the gains in the weight I could lift like he was making, but I chalked it up to just having turned 50 years old. My job wasn't to get myself back into playing shape, but rather to help light the fire in Shawn so he knew what it looked like to work out as a major college football player.

To Shawn's credit, he did the work, with great consistency, both in the weight room and in physical therapy. Over the next three months Shawn made it to fifty PT sessions with David, many of them at 6 a.m., before school. That may not sound like much to a lot of people, but 6 a.m. and Shawn had never been close friends. Especially when he had to be somewhere by himself. But Shawn motivated himself, pushed himself, and found himself getting the work done. I was proud of him and for him. It seemed to be a good sign for his future.

Little did we know that Shawn's toughest battles would be the mental ones. As difficult as the physical part is, there would be mental mountains to climb, as Coach Wilson foreshadowed in our phone call.

A Christmas Surprise

Kate and I spent two weeks with our toddlers in Pittsburgh visiting Kate's family. It is always a great time of year, and the

Dillons do Christmas big in their house. We all had a wonderful vacation.

We drove nine hours back to North Carolina, sad to be leaving family, but excited to be heading home. Exhausted, we pulled into the driveway around 11 p.m. The plan was to unbuckle the sleeping kiddos and, one by one, I would carry each child to his or her room, praying that they would transfer well and sleep through the rest of the night. I carried Leo up to bed, snuggling him under the covers. The first transfer was a success! I was headed out of the room, ready to gather up the next sleeping kid, when I was stopped dead in my tracks. On my 3-year-old's dresser was a Miller Light beer can. *What!?*

My mind raced. *Who? When? How?* You have to understand: that sort of thing just doesn't sit around in our house, and certainly not in the twins' room!

I picked it up and it was half full. I was so confused.

This wasn't a robbery, nothing appeared to be stolen, and it's not as though we had anything valuable for anyone to take anyway, save possibly the flat-screen TVs, and they were right where they normally sat.

We got all three children tucked into their beds, and Kate and I climbed into our own. She kissed me goodnight and said, "Thanks for driving us home safely, sweetie." My response was that we had something to discuss.

"Kate, you won't believe this, but I found a half-full beer can in Leo and Ella's room. I also noticed the liquor cabinet and wine refrigerator were both taped shut with duct tape."

She sat up in bed. "What? You're kidding."

I guess I was denying reality, protecting Shawn in my mind. I trusted that he was staying focused as an athlete with big dreams, even over Christmas, and wouldn't have done something like host a beer party. I said, "I have no idea what could have happened."

Kate's next words hit me with a slap of reality. "Scott, come on. You know what happened. Shawn had a party here. That's exactly what happened."

"No way. No way," I said out loud and shook my head. I was steadfast in my feeling that Shawn wouldn't do that. Not in our house. He just wouldn't make that kind of bad decision—especially at our house. And it was even more impossible that he would have let anybody go into any of the kids' rooms for any reason, I told myself. He just wouldn't do that. No way, no how.

Kate was calm. She just smiled and laughed. "He is 17, Scott. Just because you didn't do that doesn't mean he wouldn't. You were weird. He is normal. Of course he did."

I was still in disbelief.

I didn't sleep that night. At least not solid, REM sleep. It was just sort of a nap, a catnap. I couldn't wait until morning to call Shawn at his mom's house and figure out what the heck had happened.

The Phone Call

"Shawn. Dad. What's up? How's the knee? PT today?"

It was morning and he was groggy from just waking up. As I said earlier, Shawn's not a morning person, and he's not a phone guy either, so I had the double whammy going against me.

"I'm good. Just got up. I have Roskin at 2 today. How was the drive?"

"Good. Got in about 11. Listen, dude, I found a beer can half full on the kids' dresser in their room last night. Do you know anything about that?"

Long silence. I wasn't going to break it.

"Uh, yeh, well . . . I was going to talk to you about that. I had some people over the other night."

"And you were drinking?"

"No, not me. I swear."

"Who?"

"You don't know them."

"Tell me their names anyway. I need to tell their parents."

"No. It doesn't matter."

"*Doesn't matter?* Are you kidding me, Shawn?" I paused. "Did they sleep over?"

"Yeh. Some of them did. I didn't want them driving."

"Were there girls too?"

"Yeh."

"Dude. Have you lost your mind? Do you realize the kind of jeopardy you put me in, and our family? Let me paint you this picture. Headlines: 'Former UNC quarterback sued for party with alcohol leading to fatal accident.'

"And what about you, Shawn? Picture this headline: 'Star quarterback arrested for hosting party while parents are out of town.'

"And you want to be recruited, want someone to trust you with the keys to their major college program? And this is how you show responsibility?" I paused. "Does your mom know?"

"No."

"Well, tell her I will be calling her after I calm down to inform her of what you did. And she and I will come up with a discipline you deserve. I've got to hang up because I can't even talk right now. I have no idea who you are that you could do something so stupid as that, and do it in my house and to my wife and to your little brother and sisters."

And I hung up.

Meeting

I sat there across our kitchen table from Shawn. He had taken his knee brace off and had his hands clasped on the table in front of him. He knew what was coming, or so he thought. And he knew he had no choice but to sit and endure it. He had gotten good at holding his breath for as much as a day, or even two, which is the length of time he spent at our house by the visitation schedule. When he was out of line, he would just clam up until his time with us passed. I had no real authority over him to discipline or manage his behavior for extended periods. He really was only a visitor in my house through his young life.

"Dude, your mom is distraught. We are in absolute disbelief over what happened. What's up? Talk to me, man."

And he did.

And I listened.

"You have no idea what it's like to be injured. Nobody knows who you are anymore. Nobody cares. Before, I was on top of the world. Now I'm hobbling around on crutches. I can't hang out. I can't work out. I can't play basketball. Life sucks."

"What was the party about?"

"It was just me and Billy going to hang out. I even called you and you said it was OK for him to stay over."

"Yeh, I thought that was weird that you were staying at our house instead of your mom's. But I trusted you. And I thought it was weird that you would call to ask me if Billy could sleep over. But it never even crossed my mind that you would be having a party. Or that you would have alcohol in our home. I know Billy. Do his parents know? They would kill him."

"No, they don't know. Some girls got called and they came over, and when they all got here they had some beer."

"And you didn't say, 'Hey, that's not cool. Not at my dad's house. Can't do it here'?"

"No, I didn't say anything, I was just glad they showed up and we could just hang out. I duct-taped the liquor cabinet and the wine fridge so no one would get into your stuff."

"Did you drink?"

"No, I don't drink. I swear."

"Dude, it's not my life. It's yours. With all you have going for you, your future, your career, your dreams. Man, you had them all hanging out there in the balance that night by one dumb decision, and then another one to not speak up and say, 'Hey, not cool. Not at my dad's.'"

"I know." Shawn took a big pause and then let it all out. "It's just so hard. I hate it, man. It's so lonely. Nobody knows what I go through. I have no one to talk to. They don't know how big my dreams are, and they don't know how much rehab I have to do every day by myself, driving to Duke, in my room, over and over and over the same stupid stretches and lifts. I hate it."

And before I realized it, Shawn was crying.

And so was I. Except on the inside.

A parent just wants to make everything OK for his or her children. But this was a situation I couldn't make OK. Only Shawn could. This was his first "big boy" moment and challenge. His ACL injury could derail him from the future he had planned. And he was scared. And alone. And he made a bad decision.

I tried to pull the big picture together for him. "Shawn, the good news is that the worst thing didn't happen. Nobody drove and got in an accident. But this is one of those times that I hope you learn a serious lesson. You have to lead when people do things you don't agree with. They could have ruined your future. And you just sat there. You know what I mean?"

"Yeh, I know. It was stupid. I am sorry I did it."

"Well, as a man you have to accept the consequences of your behavior. That is part of growing up. It sucks, but at least you aren't in jail. Mom and I have yet to decide what will happen, but you won't be going out with anyone for a while. And I hope you use the time to get your mind right about your future and the work ahead and the lonely times in store, 'cause it's the only way through this. It will either make you or break you. And it's your choice. I love you either way. And I am here. But I hope you grow from this and it makes you stronger and more committed to your future, not less."

* * * * *

Shawn was grounded for a month. He went to school, did his PT, we lifted together a few more times that month, and I thought everything was OK and on schedule. Both Shawn's knee and his psyche seemed to be coming along fine.

Nearly a month later, it was a Friday afternoon and school was out at noon that day due to an ice storm that carried predictions of heavy snow and rain in the area that would make rush hour traffic extremely hazardous. In North Carolina, just the hint of snow will close schools because the state is not equipped to handle heavy snow or ice removal.

We had Shawn staying with us that weekend, so he texted me to say that school was getting out at noon. *Going 2 stay after and get some tutoring help. be home this afternoon*, he wrote. I looked out the window, and it had already started to hail. Based on weather predictions, I thought I had better get to the store to stock up on some milk for the kids before the really bad stuff started. I made it safely to the store, but slipped and slid on my way home. It was dangerous outside. I was nervous for Shawn staying after school for some tutoring. I texted him: *its nasty out there, where are you?* That was at 1:10 in the afternoon.

I sat down to read a book and waited for Shawn to answer and come home. The kids were upstairs napping, and the house was quiet except for the rain and hail and sleet that were pelting the roof overhead.

At 3:10, my cell phone rang. The caller ID said Shawn.

"Dad?"

"What's up?"

"Hey, my car slid off the road into a ditch. Can you come get me?"

As any parent would, I sat up, ramrod straight. "Where are you? Are you OK?"

"I'm on Highway 54 down the hill from the old McDonald's. I called Mom and she is on her way too."

"What are doing there? That's not on the way home. Just drive it out of the ditch and get home. It's a mess out there."

"Well, I was coming home this way and just hit an icy patch and slid off the road. . . . Hey, the police are here now. I gotta go."

I was ticked off. I knew where he was, and it was not along the highway he should have been taking to get to our home from school.

It didn't even register when he said, "The police are here."

I told Kate about the conversation.

"First of all, as a former school teacher, I can tell with certainty that no tutor is going to stay after school for a session when they close school early for an ice storm," she said. "That means everybody goes home."

I got even angrier. The boy was snookering me. Again. And less than a month since his last snooker, the beer party, at our home.

I put on my shoes to go get him, but as I walked across the

driveway to the car, I slipped and fell. It was really icy and dangerous. I thought, *Why would I get in the car and go up and down these unsalted roads of our neighborhoods to go and get the boy when his mom is there?* So I picked myself up and turned around and went back inside.

Thirty minutes later, still no Shawn.

My cell phone rang. The caller ID told me it was Shawn's mom.

"Scott, I am here at the scene of the accident. It's bad. Shawn's Pathfinder is upside down in the swamp at the bottom of the hill near the old McDonald's. They can't get a wrecker in here today to get it out. But it is totaled. Shawn appears to be all right, just a little bit shaken. He crawled out of the vehicle through the passenger-side window, which was smashed, because he couldn't get out his door, which was totally collapsed. The police officer said that he normally wouldn't expect to see the driver walk away from this type of flipped-car situation. . . . Shawn was lucky."

I took a deep breath after absorbing all that information.

"How is his knee?" I asked.

"He says it's OK."

"Put him on."

" . . . Hello."

"Shawn, are you OK?"

"Yeh."

"Do you need to go to the hospital?"

"No, I'm OK."

"Your knee?"

"It's fine."

"All right. I'll see you when you get here." And we ended the call.

Four o'clock . . . five o'clock . . . six o'clock. Still no Shawn.

He didn't make it to our house through the entire weekend, and it wasn't just because of the storm. He didn't want to face his dad. Not a second time.

But he would have to face himself.

And I realized that I needed help with fathering my son. It was clear that there was more to rehab than just physical exercises. His ACL wasn't the only thing torn apart and injured that November night. So were his heart and his spirit. That's what his actions were telling me. And I didn't know how to help him.

FOUR

Help Wanted: Turning to Coach

"Is there anything we can do?"

Winter, Shawn's Junior Year

"Hey, Coach, it's Scott. Happy new year, man."

"Yeh, same to you. How is our quarterback doing with rehab?"

"Well, that's why I called. I am blown away by something he did while we were in Pittsburgh over Christmas. You won't believe it."

Coach Wilson was laughing. "Go ahead, try me. I have seen a lot of stuff in my time, Scott. Shoot."

And I told him about Shawn's beer party. His denials. And then his tears and his emotions that, "Nobody knows who I am anymore and nobody cares."

"Hmmm . . . " That is all Coach said. I explained a little more about the aftermath, the talks, the discipline his mom and I imposed.

Then I shared about the accident that could have taken Shawn's life. Coach could tell how scared I was and how helpless I felt by not knowing how to help my son deal with all that was going on both in his heart and with his knee.

"Well, brother, first of all, thank God Shawn is OK. Regarding you being his father, it sounds like you and his mom handled the discipline on his ass. He needs that. You know, sometimes a good ass-whupping and strong discipline are what a young boy needs. And it makes them know they are loved. If you didn't care, you would let them get away with it. But you didn't, so you will be OK."

The accident had been a turning point for me, and it was at this point that I began my dialogue with Coach about what more we could do for Shawn.

Shawn's mother and I were not only concerned about recruiting, we also were eager to find something to pull Shawn back into focus, something that would help engage him and give him positive mental images of himself as a healthy quarterback, keeping his dreams of playing in college still intact.

* * * * *

Coach Wilson pushed his chair back from the table, folded his napkin, and set it down on the place mat in front of him. We were once again meeting at the same restaurant, Champs, in that same mall.

Coach stood up, held out his hand, and smiled. "Hi, Sue. Steve Wilson. It's nice to meet you."

Shawn's mom smiled and shook his hand. "Nice to finally meet you, too. Thanks for meeting with us today."

Coach looked across the table at Shawn, who had come with his mom, and said, "Hey quarterback, what's up? How's the rehab going?"

"Great." Shawn described a few of the details, including pool and upper-body workouts. "So, trying to put on some weight and get ready to go," he told Coach.

"Well, you look good, man. You look good."

After some talk about UNC basketball—a hot topic in late winter in North Carolina—Sue started right in. "Coach, we are really frustrated, and we have no idea what to do to get Shawn exposure and help get him recruited. And that's why I wanted to meet with you. Can you help us?"

Coach paused for just a moment before beginning. "Well, I don't know if I can help you, but I can tell you what I do know. And that is this: your son is a very good player, one of the best I have seen in my career, and I have been around a long time. What he does on film is rare to someone who knows what they are looking at in a quarterback.

"But I have also been disappointed by the lack of attention his dad tells me he is receiving from colleges. I don't have any explanation. It's possible that his knee injury has scared everybody off, but today an ACL is not as devastating as it was twenty years ago, and lots of guys come back stronger than ever.

"So to try and get some perspective, I've called around to get an opinion on Shawn's films from some of my NFL and college contacts and asked them for their evaluation. They all confirmed my instincts. Shawn can play.

"Now, will he get the chance to play in college? Of course he will. Will he have a selection of colleges to choose from? He should. But I can't guarantee that. But you all need to remember this: you can only go to one school. So all the recruiting hype and attention is overrated, and at the end of the day it's noise and nonsense that often hinders the development of a player because they actually start to believe the hype.

"Now, here is the good news." Coach turned his attention directly to Shawn. "Shawn, you don't have that problem. Because you don't have any hype. And in a way that's good, because it makes you hungry and makes you focused. And it will take all your hunger and focus to become the player you are capable of becoming."

Coach then turned back to Sue and me. "I know what I see on his tape and I don't need anybody to tell me how many stars he has." (This is a recruiting system that gives certain players higher or lower numbers of stars.) "I can see talent for myself. When I was in the college coaching game, I never relied on those stars. I relied on my own evaluations. We took one- and two-star kids [lower-rated players] and made them All-Americans and NFL prospects."

Coach was far from done. We were getting a behind-the-scenes look at what goes on inside the mind of a top football evaluator. And it was becoming clear that Coach was already on Shawn's side, working hard for him. I didn't know if Shawn could appreciate this at that moment, but it was quite a gift Coach was giving him.

Coach continued. "So, no doubt about it, Shawn is behind the curve and has an uphill battle and will have to make his move from under the radar. He is damaged goods." Those words stung, but we had to hear them. "And he doesn't have prototype size, and in his film he does not show a big, strong dropback arm where the ball flies out of his hand fifty yards down the field. Those things, too, are working against him.

"But what he does have is creativity, athleticism, and accuracy. And when he plays he has fun—and that is contagious. You have to watch him play, because he may do something you have never seen before."

Coach paused to take a sip of his drink and catch his breath. Shawn's mom wanted to step in, so she was next to speak.

"But Coach, why are you the only one who thinks this? You and his dad. Are you both crazy?"

"I'm not. I can't speak for his dad, but I'm not." Coach chuckled at this soft-pedal approach at humor; he has this delightful way about him. "I've had my evaluation confirmed by a former quarterback coach in the Pac 12 [conference] and another one from the Big Ten. But the fact of the matter is that Shawn is going to have to change some other peoples' minds with his play next fall. And his options will be limited because quarterbacks commit to schools this spring, so some schools won't even be looking at quarterbacks in his class anymore come June. It's not the ideal situation, but you have to play the hand you are dealt."

Now it was my turn. "So Coach, what should we do? Is there anything that we can be doing from now until next season that can help Shawn?"

"Good question. And the answer is yes, there is. Playing quarterback in college is a lot less about how well you throw the ball—because you wouldn't be there if you didn't have some arm talent—and a whole lot more about your knowledge of the game, both offensively and defensively. If Shawn wants to impress colleges with his play next year, it will not only be with his physical skills, but also with his decision-making and his understanding of the game."

"How does he get that?" I asked. "Look, here's my honest assessment. I don't think that's going to come at the high school level."

"That's OK. It rarely does," Coach said.

And then came the key moment.

"You see, in life, when you don't get what you want, it's important that you step back and make sure you go out and get what you need. That is what I am talking about: a quarterback class that we would do once or twice a week depending on his rehab and schoolwork schedule. We squirrel away and sit down and go over Football 101, from A to Z, and learn the game itself from the inside out.

"You see, what most people fail to realize is that there is only one game of football. It's played at many different levels, but in the end, the field is the same—120 yards long and 53 yards wide—and each team has eleven players who can only line up so many different ways.

"Learn the game, and you can play it at any level. Learn the game, and you will understand it for the rest of your life.

"It's like playing chess. You would never enter a chess tournament, especially a high-level competition, without knowing what all the pieces can do and how they work together and against each other, would you? Of course not. At least, not if you hoped to win.

"So, as a quarterback, if you learn the game and can play it like chess . . . well, Shawn can then separate himself from every other high school quarterback in America. And combined with his physical talent, he will get to go to school and play where he wants to, and get a great education for free. And that's the goal, isn't it?"

We were all a bit flabbergasted.

"Absolutely," Shawn's mom said.

Then Coach looked across the table at Shawn. "So, quarterback, if you had your choice of any schools in the country, what would be your top five?"

Shawn smiled, realizing he had a clean slate to throw out his dream schools. Now it was his turn to speak. "Vanderbilt would be my number one school. Play in the SEC, get a big-time education, and do it in Nashville, 'cause I love country music."

"OK, OK," Coach said. "Who else?"

"Well, last year I went to the Clemson camp, and they noticed me, and Coach Sweeney pulled me aside and said they would be watching me. So I like them, and I like their offense, the way they use the quarterback. It's a big-time program and a big-time stadium, so I would like to go there if I could.

"And I like the new coach at N.C. State, and I know my mom and dad probably couldn't see me being a Wolfpack guy, but I could, so they would have to just deal with it." Shawn glanced over at us and smiled.

"OK, go on."

"I like ECU [East Carolina University]. They have a great offense, and it's close to home and I feel like I might be able to play early in my career. And I also like Wake Forest a little. It's close and in the ACC, and it's a good education."

"So, as of today, that's your top five," Coach said. "OK, good. Well, we've got some work to do—*you've* got work to do—to make those viable options. But I like your picks. And I can tell you and your parents that you have the talent to play at any of those schools, no question about it. But getting the *opportunity* is what you need, and that's what we have to work on."

I was ready for what Coach was offering. "So, when can we get started with this quarterback class?" I asked.

"You tell me. I'm available whenever you want me to be available."

"Shawn?" I asked.

"I can go on Tuesday night at seven, after PT."

"OK, my house, basement, at 7," I said, looking at Shawn and Coach. Both nodded.

The first quarterback class was set.

FIVE

The Class

"Learn the one game at its highest level"

March

It was Tuesday evening and me, Kate, Shawn, and our kiddos were all sitting around the dinner table. There was a knock at the back door. Benson, the family golden retriever, started to bark and ran to the door, tail wagging.

I got up and opened the door. Coach Wilson walked in, carrying his projector over one shoulder and his laptop computer over the other. He had on an EA SPORTS baseball cap, shorts, and golf shirt. His bright smile and "Hello everybody!" put everyone in the room at ease. Coach always had a fantastic way with kids. Shawn's brother, Leo, and sisters Ella and Jordan turned around from their tuna casserole and sheepishly smiled back at this big persona standing by the table.

Shawn rose and walked over to shake hands with Coach. "You ready to go, big man?"

Shawn smiled. "You bet."

Three men headed downstairs: Shawn first, taking each step with care since he was still rehabbing his reconstructed knee,

Coach Wilson, and then me.

Coach had played both offense and defense in the National Football League, something few men can boast. He'd played for the Dallas Cowboys at wide receiver and the Denver Broncos at defensive back at a time, the late 1970s and early to mid-1980s, when those teams were reaching Super Bowls and thus at the pinnacle of a wildly growing sport. He'd gone on to be a successful college coach at Howard University (1989-2001), his alma mater, then coached at Bowie State and Texas Southern University. He'd earned many accolades as a coach: MEAC Coach of the Year, twice ('89, '93), had an undefeated team and conference champion in 1993, and in 2003 led a Bowie State team that boasted a defense so fierce and dominating that it was credited with "the greatest overall statistical performance in CIAA conference history." He'd been a mentor and father figure to hundreds of young men, including a talented quarterback, Jay Walker, who was *Sports Illustrated*'s Division I-AA Player of the Year (1993) and would go on to be a Maryland state Delegate and ESPN football color analyst; and Pep Hamilton, who had helped build Stanford football with star quarterback Andrew Luck and was the offensive coordinator of the NFL's Indianapolis Colts.

In short, Shawn probably had little to no appreciation of who this man was and how golden an opportunity it would be to sit at the feet of and learn from someone who had both played and coached as much football, from both sides of the ball, as nearly anyone alive.

Coach Wilson began to set up his projector, facing a basement concrete wall; simple, but it would work. As he set up, Coach chitchatted with Shawn, asking about the rehab work on his knee and how his schoolwork was going. Once his projector bulb was warmed up and his Internet connection established, Coach Wilson got right down to work. This was Class One.

The information flew, much of it technical talk about playing quarterback at the highest level. Coach had numerous gems for Shawn:

- "You don't want the quarterback dirty, or even hit! He's too valuable. The quarterback must agree and participate in his own protection."

- "Name the last running quarterback that won the Super Bowl." (Shawn and I had no answer for that one.) (If you're wondering: both Steve Young of the 49ers and Seattle's Russell Wilson could run, but it was their pocket management and "escape-ability" that earned them Super Bowl victories, not their running abilities.)

- "Remember: you can't win the game in the first quarter, only the fourth. . . . You can't win the championship game in September, only in December. . . . We must protect ourselves with our eyes *and* our head—not just our feet. . . . . Shawn, you've got to understand that 75 percent of the play is executed mentally *pre*-snap, before the ball ever leaves the center's hands. That makes the game slower, simpler. It makes you faster, more efficient, and unstoppable. It can make you a nightmare for *any* defense in *any* league, at any level."

- "The quarterback must learn the defense! Every defense has a structural weakness. You must probe it, and take advantage of it, so that no matter what they do, they are 'wrong.'"

The lessons and the teaching went on. Both Shawn and I listened carefully, mesmerized as Coach taught.

- "The quarterback: if you are responsible for *winning* the game, then you must manage the winning process, which includes scoring points—and preventing points. Because it is very difficult for the opponent to score if they don't have the ball. . . . Ball possession—what I call the ten-yard fight—is the secret to championship football."

- "The quarterback must know the defender's conflicts and exploit them. A single defender on every play has to address his conflict of having two distinct jobs to do—to defend both the run and pass. But he can only do one!"

The terms flew from Coach, phrases like "coverage leverage" and "MOFO" (middle of the field open) and "high access."

I wrote down and summarized the key words from session one: *offensive philosophy, MOFO, the second-man-through concept,* and more.

After a while, we reached a point where Coach could see he was slowly losing Shawn's ability to take in much more; they had covered an awful lot in just one session. It was then that Coach did something that pulled Shawn's attention fully back: he put on Shawn's highlight DVD from his junior season. That perks up any young man watching film: suddenly, it's a highlight reel of yourself. Shawn readjusted in his seat and settled back. These were Shawn's best plays, his "wow" plays, and we looked at them given the lecture and notes we had just taken.

I never expected the discussion to lead where it went. Coach played the first three of Shawn's top plays from that junior year, all TDs. Here was Coach breaking down the second of them: "It's MOFO, hard squat . . . the QB catches the snap, takes a three-step drop with a big crossover, gets to a depth of nine yards, but the offensive linemen can't protect that deep of a pocket. So QB has to hitch up three times and fires a strike for a TD."

Looks impressive, I thought, just as I'd seen it that night in the stands, and I'm sure Shawn had to smile a bit to relive that TD throw again. But what Coach said next stopped us both: "Good. But the perfect play would have been to take a two-step drop, one step up, and fire the same throw for the TD. . . . That would be less dramatic, simpler, and easier."

Coach was just beginning to teach us how to read defenses through the eyes of an advanced football mind.

And then Coach stopped: "That's enough for today." And just like that, Shawn had a whole new world opened up for him. Coach asked me what I thought. I answered that I couldn't believe there was that much to learn from three of Shawn's very best plays from last year.

"Oh, there is plenty to learn. We're just getting started. But I wanted to show Shawn that our standard for playing quarterback is much higher than anything he has ever seen. There is only one game of football. If you learn it *at its highest level* then you will equip yourself to play at any level. Not a lot of people understand that, or want to understand that, and they want to argue that the NFL game is too sophisticated for high school, but that's simply not true. There is *one game*. Become an expert of the one game and it will serve you the rest of your life."

Class 2: Know Where to Find the Information You Need

Key terms and teaching points covered: *press-the-release technique . . . back shoulder . . . SKY . . . cloud . . . sink . . . snapshots . . . a Drew Brees film study*

The next get-together went similar to the first class. It was a week later, and all three of us were seated in the same spots. Coach dove right into teaching, not even waiting for his projector to warm up.

- "I have strong opinions about the game because I lived it. I played wide receiver in college, and after one year as a wide receiver with the Dallas Cowboys, Tom Landry [the legendary Cowboys coach of the 1970s and '80s] says to me, 'We need you to convert to defense, or you won't make the team.' So I did, and I played the next two seasons at cornerback with the Cowboys and then seven more with the Broncos."

- "The quarterback must learn to work and compute information from *snapshots*. . . . A quarterback is never going to be able to track a defensive back through his entire drop. But it's not necessary. Take a snapshot of the defense during the pre-snap, execute the play-fake, take a drop, then turn your eyes to the same photo and take a second snapshot, and then quickly compute the information."

- "We will work on three distinct areas to improve as a quarterback, and they are mechanics and footwork, knowledge of defenses, and the speed of your processor. And the one we are going to emphasize most is having a working knowledge of defense—as if you were a defensive coordinator. Mastery comes when, as a quarterback, you know what the defense is supposed to do by rule, and then use it against them. That is when the game gets really fun, but not many quarterbacks ever learn enough to be able to play at that level. That is what we are after."

Soon Coach was breaking away from the nuts and bolts of football and talking about life. "Shawn, let me tell you a story about when I was in high school. We used to drive our cars around town on Friday nights in the summertime and impress the girls. We would drive slowly up to this one railroad track crossing and then peel out and burn rubber, and we thought we were hot stuff. One night, as I peeled out, I dropped the clutch on my Chevy. Man, was I embarrassed. So we got the car to my grandfather's house and he put it up on the blocks in his garage. I asked, 'Grandpa, can you help me fix my clutch?' And I told him what happened. He said he would.

"After we got the car up on the blocks, he walked to the door, stood in the entrance, and said, 'Steve, take it apart, *pay attention,* and then put it back together.' And then he walked out. And that's how I learned about cars."

And then Coach bridged his story back to football.

- "You gotta know where to look for the information you need. The starting point is the key. And that is whether the middle of the field is open or closed during pre-snap. Tom Landry always emphasized that. What I am teaching comes from my personal experience, first as a Cowboy wide receiver for [Hall of Fame quarterback] Roger Staubach, and then the next year as a defensive back *defending* quarterback Danny White and [wide receivers] Drew Pearson and Tony Hill [of the Cowboys]. I needed information and I needed it fast, or my pro career would be a short one. So I had to find it for myself, and a lot of it I already knew from my years as a wide receiver."

I was taking notes furiously and hardly looked up. Shawn had his pen and pad out and was scribbling a few things himself. But mostly, in truth, the information just washed over him. I am certain he was not sure what it all meant or where to put it in his mind's filing system.

The amount of information necessary to be an elite quarterback is massive, but more important is the ability to process and manipulate the information within nanoseconds, and then make the proper decision and execute the appropriate throw physically. There was way more to quarterbacking excellence than I had ever realized, even though I had three years of NFL experience under Dan Reeves, Mike Shanahan, and Don Shula. Coach was breaking it down to the smallest detail so that it could be digested and reconstructed.

Coach went on to finish the session by pulling up some video on the New Orleans Saints' All-Pro, Drew Brees. We looked at ten plays of Brees and his drops and footwork in the pocket. Coach would stop the film after nearly every step and ask what could be gleaned from each "snapshot" on the screen. Coach wanted Shawn to learn to process information like an NFL pro. (Brees was a great choice, I thought. I personally have been a huge Drew Brees fan, not only as a quarterback but also as a man. I had read his book, *Coming Back Stronger,* and was inspired by his perseverance and tenacity to come back from an ACL tear his junior year in high school. Brees had also overcome being under-recruited and became All-Big Ten and eventually won a Super Bowl after being written off, following a shoulder reconstruction, by the rest of the league. So when Coach put up Brees as the model for Shawn, I couldn't have been more pleased.)

Next, Coach put on film of college great Johnny Manziel of Texas A&M. We watched plays from his game against Alabama, an upset win for A&M that earned "Johnny Football" national attention and set the stage for the Heisman trophy campaign. We watched his famous play, the one in which he fumbled the ball in the pocket, retrieved it, rolled left, and then threw back across his body—something extremely difficult to do—to a wide open receiver in the end zone.

But when Coach replayed the video, he pointed out that what should have happened was Manziel should have caught the snap, turned his feet, and fired a strike to his slot receiver on the slant; this receiver was wide open and the play would have resulted in the same touchdown, only without all the drama. Coach walked us through several other plays, and we saw the same conclusion. And then—just for emphasis, it seemed—Coach projected Shawn's highlight video on the same wall against which we had just seen Brees and Manziel. And Coach then proceeded to take plays four through six of Shawn's highlights and break them down, just like he had in the first session, and just like he had done for Brees and Manziel. Same wall. Same wisdom. Same standard.

We watched a play which was a "smash route," which is a combination of a short route by the wide receiver and then a corner route by the slot receiver, and is designed to defeat a Cover 2 defense. Shawn took a nice, deep drop, planted his back foot, and fired a strike to his slot receiver, who caught the ball and tiptoed out of bounds for a first down. Impressive. But Coach rewound the video and said, "Here are the coaching points: the drop is too deep. If you set at nine yards deep [as Shawn did], that puts too much stress on our offensive linemen. When throwing left, a quarterback must drive the ball into a firm left leg. I don't see that with you, Shawn. I see more of a rotary emphasis to generate power; that is residual from when you were a boy. As a youngster, when you aren't strong enough to drive the ball like a grown man, this is how most young men first learn to throw. But now, driving the ball requires opening up the hips more and having a firm left side and driving into a bent front knee."

OK, I thought. *That's a pretty astute observation, and necessary for Shawn to know.* I wouldn't have been able to detect that; after all, it looked like a perfect ball to me.

And Coach went on to do this with the fifth and sixth highlights. On the last one, a beautiful strike to the corner of the end zone for a touchdown, I said to myself, *What could possibly be wrong with that throw?*

But Coach rewound the video and commented: "OK, with MOFO [middle of the field open], you need to realize that short-side money in the boundary is better interest than to the field. Look at the boundary safety [with the ball on a hash mark, the field is divided into a wide side and a shorter side, the boundary]: he starts on the hash, and he stays there, so we know he can't get to the sideline to cover the outside vertical." And it went on, where Coach showed Shawn that he actually missed a higher percentage play, an easier play that also would have likely been a touchdown. The pass he threw scored, but if he had missed the throw slightly, it wouldn't have. Coach talked about the difference, and wrapped it up by saying, "*That* is great quarterbacking." And he meant taking the higher-percentage, easier play. Every time.

The class was over, and I was overwhelmed by the depth of Coach Wilson's teaching.

And what was amazing was it didn't feel like criticism or degrading to have Coach critique Shawn's film. It was like he was letting us in on the secrets of the game at another level.

What was important to Shawn and me was that we were left hungry for more.

Class 3: Take Pride in Your Work

Key terms: *pro set . . . slot set . . . core receivers . . . COV 1 . . . COV 3 . . . backer/bronco force . . . BASE pass protection*

"Shawn, I was talking to Pep [Hamilton] the other day and he reminded me of something that I need you to embrace: *Quarterback is a lifestyle. And it is non-negotiable. You aren't playing quarterback, you* are *a quarterback.* And I need you to know what that means and to live the *lifestyle.* It's not for everybody. The question is, 'Is it for you?' And only you can answer that.

"The lifestyle means a different method of making decisions, of how you invest your time, of your attitude and perspective on everything you do. Let me tell you a story about my grandfather, who was a Baptist preacher in northern Durham with a second grade education. He was one of the smartest men I ever knew.

"Every Saturday night he would make me shine his shoes, rubbing in the black shoe polish for five minutes and then buffing it out to a spit shine. People don't do that anymore, but my grandfather was fanatical about his shoes. And every Sunday morning he would call me into his room before going to service and he would take his shoes off and hold them up to the light and say, 'I can see a scuff you missed here. Give them one more shine for me, would you?' Man, I hated doing that, and I swear most mornings there wasn't a tarnish on his shoe; he was just making me do it again for him. That is the way he was. And one day I asked him about it, and he told me, 'Steve, you can wear a ragtag suit and an old tie, but if you stand up in front of a group and your shoes are shined, they will respect you. That is why I have you pay attention to detail for me, because when the church sees my shoes shined, they know they can take my words seriously.'"

Coach looked at Shawn and said, "Shawn, you've got to take pride in your work, in every little thing you do from here on out. I call it 'a little bit more.' You have to do everything you can every day to become the best you can be. And when you do that, then you have to do a little bit more. That is what I want you to learn how to do. OK?"

Coach provided an illustration from his own playing career. He was in rookie camp with the Cowboys—along with nearly three hundred other players—and was in the wide receiver line. For the first two days Steve Wilson never got to run any routes because the line was in alphabetical order, and the coaches never got to the Ws before the passing part of practice would end. So, after practice, Steve would stay and run his routes against air, by himself. The second day he did that, Roger Staubach came over and asked what he was doing. Steve answered, "I am working on my routes so I can be ready for the next team I try out for, because I haven't gotten any work here." Staubach called for some balls and started throwing routes to the rookie wide receiver one on one. From that moment on, Steve Wilson was on his way to making the team. *All you can do, and then a little bit more.*

Coach then went to the computer and his projector and pulled up his website, Ultimate Football University, and began to scroll though folders and subfolders and files on the screen of playbooks and videos and diagrams. It was amazing and a bit over-whelming. I asked Coach, "What is that?" and he told Shawn and me that it was all the information he had collected over his 35-year career, all "libraried" in one place, his UFU site. Shawn and I didn't say anything. We just looked at the screen as if staring at Mount Everest or having just walked into the Library of Congress.

Coach then took us to a page on the site titled "History of Ultimate Football University." And he scrolled through his personal family tree of coaches and players he had been exposed to in his career and through his father's career. It was like a Who's Who of the NFL Hall of Fame, from Johnny Unitas to Jim Brown, from Tom Landry to Bill Walsh. It was amazing how many people had affected Coach Wilson's career and how that influence was being offered to Shawn.

Coach laughed and began to tell another story. "When I coached at Howard, I would make one of my quarterbacks carry a big duffel bag that was filled with old VCR tapes to every meeting we had every day. The guys used to joke about it because it was so heavy. They wondered why I would need all those tapes, and the answer was obvious to me: if there was a play or a video that I needed to look at, I would never be without access to it. Pep had to carry it the most, I think, and he ended up calling it 'the big bag theory.' I heard him speak at a clinic recently and he laughed as he told the story and said that he doesn't have a big bag himself because he just sends everything he needs saved to me and he knows it will be properly filed and available to him whenever he needs it. He carries around a computer tablet nowadays and has access to all the same information, because like me, he never, ever wanted to be caught without having access to his library of football information."

Coach was teaching Shawn so much about respecting the history of the game. He talked about the importance of studying the game, in the present, but also with an appreciation for the past. He referenced the earliest 500-yard passing games, put up by guys like Norm Van Brocklin and Bob Waterfield, and then the advent of the Packer "power sweep," the run and shoot, the H-back, the spread offense, the wishbone option, zone read, and pistol formations. And he was telling Shawn to realize they are all related, and then to understand what defenses did to adjust and adapt to each new craze of offense. The game has a natural ebb and flow, Coach said, as each side adjusts to new techniques and tactics by the other.

Class 4: Control the Controllables

Key terms and teaching points: *see the game in pictures . . . mental reps . . . MOFC (middle of the field closed) . . . Pick 'n Stick . . . the importance of footwork*

The weather was turning to spring, the flowers starting to bloom, and the workouts in rehab began moving outdoors and onto the track. We also began to plan for which combine events Shawn could attend and perform at for college evaluations.

The unspoken truth of the matter was that Shawn's mom and I remained disappointed, even discouraged, that more mail and interest was not materializing from colleges after Shawn's stellar junior season.

In this next class, Coach Wilson chose to address that situation directly with Shawn.

- "Shawn, congratulations. It appears that you are ahead of schedule with the physical rehab on your knee, and I can see you are bulking up. The key here is to keep on focusing on the control of what we can control, and not allow focus on anything *outside* of our control, like scholarship offers to other players or recruiting rankings or marketing."

- "Now remember, I've had the top talent evaluators look at your film, and they agree with me, and I am excited. I don't want you to panic about scholarships. This is what will happen: you will have a super senior season in high school, earn a scholarship, and then at some point, somebody is going to give you the ball in college football to be their quarterback, and when you get it, you will *never give it back*, not until your career is over! That is what we are preparing for . . . " Coach stopped. He knew I was in the room. "And although your dad may object to such a lofty goal at this stage of your career, I am here to suggest that you might not be done after college."

Coach paused. The silence was meant to allow this to sink in for both of us. He was planting seeds. After a moment, he went right back into class mode and began teaching again.

- "Remember, the number one job of a quarterback is to win, and no matter the stats, if you don't win, then coaches get fired. And to win, it's not about stats, it's about your ability to manage an offense, manipulate a defense, and score points. And it's about the 10-yard fight . . . first downs and ball control!"

- "Regarding your combines upcoming: remember, the 40 [-yard dash] time is used as just one evaluation, but it has nothing to do with *quarterbacking*. But whatever time you run, it needs to be your best, so don't run until you are ready to put up a fast number!"

- "Shawn, you should be starting to see the game in pictures . . . remember: MOFO, MOFC [middle of the field closed], a hard-squat cornerback, a head-up, press-the-release cornerback . . . remember all of this."

- "You do not have to physically play the game to improve, Shawn. You can improve *mentally by doing reps in your mind* and going through them in the film room. All of this practice makes you faster—not on your feet, but in your mind, in the computer processor that is your football mind. Our goal is to have you playing at the speed of a junior in college next year!"

That seemed astounding to both Shawn and me, but you have to know Coach. He wouldn't have said it if he didn't think it was possible. For Shawn's mental state to be advanced three to four years past his actual physical age, well, that felt like a daunting task, but it was the standard coach was setting.

- "When the quarterback is throwing against man-to-man coverage, there is no real progression. It is about this: pick your best matchup and best leverage and *fire!*" Coach called this 'Pick 'n Stick.' "If you pick the wrong one, scramble, because you will be late if you try to pick up another receiver and throw it off his break!"

Now Coach was back into the quarterback determining the matchup he wants. He talked about digesting the information pre-snap, confirming that information within the first couple of steps back, and then firing on time to a route breaking away from leverage. Next we were into things like "double bump/press situations" and the importance of developing a common language and communication among coaches and players.

- "Great quarterback footwork is like a mountain goat—the goat doesn't look down at the mountain, but it is sure-footed! And the quarterbacks at the highest level are always working on their footwork, even a guy like Cam Newton of the Carolina Panthers, as pure an athletic talent as the NFL has. [Newton is Shawn's favorite pro quarterback, by the way.] But he needs to work on his feet, and his balance, to become more consistent and accurate before he can become elite as a quarterback!"

Before long we were packing away notebooks and video equipment and it was time to head to bed for the evening. Both Coach and Shawn headed out for the night.

* * * * *

Over the next couple of days I reviewed my notes from the previous classes, and I was blown away that I had taken more than 40 pages of notes from class with Coach—in just four classes! I wrote down everything: the stories, the technical terms, the concepts, everything. My mind went back to my NFL career, and I didn't remember ever getting this much information, even at that level. So the next day I asked Coach Wilson about that.

"Scott, that's a great question. And the truth is that what we are going over wasn't something you would have been taught during an NFL season. This information is learned in the off-season when you don't have to prepare for games.

"A lot of my coaching philosophy was influenced by two men, Coach Landry and Dan Reeves. The reality is I played nine of my ten seasons on teams coached by Dan. He is a guy that should be in the NFL Hall of Fame when you look at his resume. He coached the Broncos in two Super Bowls and the [Atlanta] Falcons in one, and he played in three Super Bowls as a player. He was NFL Coach of the Year with the Giants and the Falcons.

"Dan and I always got along, and I know you had a good relationship with him too. Let me tell you why I think that was: because Dan was one of us, a free agent who beat the odds and had a long NFL career as a player and coach. And Dan reflected Coach Landry; they were both fanatical about the littlest details on both sides of the ball. That greatly influenced my coaching and teaching, and it's what you see in our classes."

Class 5: The Challenge

Key terms and teaching points: *Breakoff . . . hot reads . . . the 'Pistol' philosophy . . . the "kill" audible package . . . studying Colin Kaepernick on film . . . the 49ers' quarterback school agenda*

Reassembled in the basement, it was quickly apparent that Coach was ready to turn this visit toward a much bigger picture for Shawn. Coach had earned Shawn's trust and confidence, and now he fully had his attention.

- "I need to change your mind-set, Shawn. This isn't about a scholarship. You will get a scholarship; this is about getting a job! When you get to college, there will be three guys ahead of you with scholarships, and all in the same boat. This is about getting the job, ahead of them, and never letting go of it!"

- "You are in a deficit situation now, but one day, soon, like within 18 months, you will be in the college game. And you can never assume it's even or fair; we can't assure you that a college coach will like you, or whether some rich alumnus will want his kid or this or that kid to play. The key to all this is *information!* If you have info the others don't have, you win! If you can get info they can't get, you win! A mentor of mine told me: if you have money, you can buy information, but if you have information, you can make money!"

- "Your ability to find the information, to process it and act on it, will separate you from all others! And once you have the internal processor going on, like a computer's CPU, you either use it, or you abuse it, and the latter will mean you didn't apply it. Here's an example: you'll end up saying things in a film session like, 'Damn, that was a hot read . . . I knew that, that the back could only get one of the linebackers, and that was a "hot," but I got sacked and fumbled . . . ' Not good. You abused the information you had."

- "Shawn, to be honest, I am trying to ram a huge amount of information down your throat so that you will regurgitate it back to me. And that it will come up every time. The more you can swallow now, the better you will be in the long run!"

It was becoming apparent to me that these principles work in *anything* in life. Lack key information? Playing guesswork with your job? None of that will serve you well. I could see it in real estate, in football, in life, in anything. Ask questions. Be humble. Tell others you don't know this or that piece of information, but would like to learn it. From *them.*

- "I was a head coach for twenty years, and let me tell you something: the quarterback who gets this stuff first, gets the ball first. That doesn't mean he will keep it. But he will get first crack."

- "I once had a redshirt freshman quarterback throw six picks [interceptions] in a game, and he came to the sideline, took a knee beside me with a tear rolling down his cheek, and said, 'Please, Coach, get me out of here.' And you know what I told him, Shawn? I told him that he got me into this situation, so he was going to get me out of it! And the next year, Ted 'Sweet Flight' White's sophomore season, he led the entire country at every level, in passing efficiency and quarterback rating, and threw 36 touchdowns! If you look at things the right way, Shawn, pain can be turned into gain."

- "Shawn, it's already April. And in September the bullets fly for real in high school games that count in your career. That's coming quick. Now you haven't lost one yet, have you? Good. Plan on keeping it that way."

- "When I played, I was obsessed. I thought about this stuff every day, every hour. I had to, Shawn. I wasn't the most physically gifted. Your dad was the same way. And the guys you are going to compete with in your future are obsessed too. So the mental part of things counts for a lot, because most guys don't have access to this part of being a quarterback, or they get access late. You have a huge advantage in these sessions, if you use it!"

- "When I watch your junior year film, I see you making plays when five [defensive] guys break loose into the backfield, and you still make the play. Our goal is that you don't have to do that as much. You still *can*, but because of your mind and its football processor, you can't be blitzed, they can't play coverage, they can't be in the wrong run defense . . . you just always rip them a new one no matter what they do, and then you're just chuckling. 'That was too easy!' you say to yourself. Now *that's* the goal."

Calling Shawn Out

Coach paused for a moment. With what came next, I wasn't entirely sure what he was reading. Maybe Shawn wasn't showing enough excitement over this information that was being laid out before him . . . maybe Coach could see Shawn was getting it, but that he wasn't showing enough fire. Or appreciation. Or something. The important thing is what came next. It didn't really have to do with football. Coach had a new message to deliver.

"Shawn, at this point, I need to see your *fire*, to see your fire for this stuff. And see you begin the process of becoming a professional at the position of quarterback. Or, go play basketball. It's basically that simple, son." With that out there, Coach went on.

"Let me tell you both a story. When I was a little boy, I remember watching the first Super Bowl on TV. And after the game, I went into the kitchen and ripped open a big brown paper bag from the grocery store. I took some crayons and I wrote on that bag: 'Someday I will play in a Super Bowl!' I had totally forgotten I had ever done that, until one Sunday in 1987, when I ran out onto the grass of the Rose Bowl for Super Bowl Twenty-One [XXI]. My mom had brought that paper bag to show me the day before we played the game! I stood there in the end zone, just awestruck that I was really there, living my childhood dream, something I had written down on a grocery bag.

"That's what I want for you too, Shawn, to help you live your dream.

"I can't make you learn the information, but I can put it all around and make it available to you, and that is what I am doing. It's up to you to learn this because, in the end, it isn't taught, it's learned. And you have to really want to go after the pursuit and mastery of this stuff to get it all. It's not something that comes to you passively; you have to go out and get it with an uncommon passion. Are you willing to do that?"

To emphasize his point, Coach Wilson then shared some of the San Francisco 49ers' quarterback school agenda. Part of the day's breakdown showed classroom work from 10 a.m. to noon and then again from 1 to 4 p.m. in the afternoon. "That's a long day of studying, Shawn! A quarterback is another coach! Shawn, can you pay attention that long? Could you do it for $5 million a year? If you want to, you gotta start now. You've got to be able to expand your classroom focus to more than just thirty minutes!"

It was clear that the mental game is so much more than most people think, or even imagine. So much of what Coach was preaching to Shawn about football seemed so true of nearly anything in life: your approach, your attitude, your preparation—

that is what determines so much. Coach said he was teaching in a way that he had coined as "stack learning." He had found great success over the years by teaching the student what they had already partially learned! As an example, I had watched many times where Coach used terms and words in conversation with Shawn that he had not yet defined! I would think: *Has he defined that term yet, did I miss it? . . . I think I know what that means, but I don't want to appear dumb . . .* And the conversation would go on, and there appeared to be a hole in the dialogue of understanding or overall flow. And then, in the next session, or later in the same class, he would offer the definition of that term! And as a learner, you think to yourself, *Oh, I already know that concept, but now I have a formal definition! OK, that really makes sense to me now.* It's like Coach Wilson has a black belt in teaching, in guiding the learner through learning.

* * * * *

Over that next weekend, Shawn had been cleared to run and, therefore, to take drops and make throws. So Coach Wilson took him to the turf field at Duke University and put him through some drills. It was so exciting to see for me as a father. Here was Shawn, dropping and throwing the football again. It was springtime—in every way. Not only were the flowers blooming, but it seemed that Shawn was back to being himself as a young man, shedding the doubt and anxiety about his future and working his butt off to become the best quarterback he could be in preparation for a memorable senior year. I was proud of him and I could see him committed to the process both physically and mentally, doing the work on both fronts.

In fact, I noticed that it was hard for me to physically keep up at times with the pace of the workouts and the classroom sessions. I felt worn out some days, and Shawn actually had more juice than me, which was unusual up to this point in our lives, but I was glad to see it. It was about time, and after all, he didn't have to help chase his three toddler siblings around the house—I was doing that.

SIX

From Madden to More Classwork

"It's not what somebody else says to you, but what you say to yourself, that will make the difference"

Spring, End of Shawn's Junior Year

It's in the Game

It was late in one of the spring classes. It had been an intense session as far as the amount of information that was covered, and the group needed a break mentally if not physically. I left to check on Kate and the kiddos upstairs, and when I came back Coach Wilson was hooking up another machine to the wall and mumbling how he was going to teach Shawn a lesson and that it had probably been a long time since the boy had experienced a butt-whupping like he was about to get.

Shawn was sitting there smiling and grinning and acting all cocky, and I wasn't sure what was going on.

Turns out that in my short absence Shawn had mentioned that he was beating up all of his buddies on the Internet on Madden® NFL Football and that no one wanted to play him anymore because he was too good. And so—and I could see it from across the room—sly like a fox, Coach Wilson lured him into the challenge of playing against him. The friendly trash talk had begun.

I didn't say anything, because as far as that kind of video gaming and technology, I refer to myself as a dinosaur, and I am not much interested in changing at this stage in my life. I had tried when I first got Shawn the Madden console, thinking it would be a way for us to connect as father and son, but when he put that controller in my hand and I couldn't make it work very well and he was making it sing like Springsteen on a sweet guitar riff . . . well, I have to be honest: I lost interest.

Coach and Shawn kept jabbering back and forth as the video came up on the wall. I watched as they each picked their team: Shawn the Carolina Panthers and Coach Wilson the Broncos. They started their game. Shawn had the ball first and the screen flashed with Xs and Os and charts and graphs, and then the view of the line of scrimmage would come up, just like a real game on TV, except it was all animated. And if you've seen this, you know how it goes, but for those who haven't, allow me: the on-screen voices call the cadence and the ball is snapped and the avatars run the play and the defensive players respond. It's pretty much real-life tackling with regard to sound and action.

Shawn's Panthers, and a very lifelike quarterback Cam Newton, got crushed in the first series; Shawn had to punt. Coach Wilson's Broncos got the ball and reeled off eight straight running plays, marching the ball down the field for a touchdown.

Shawn offered this: "Are you scared to throw it, Coach?"

"I don't have to. Not when you can't stop the run."

Shawn's Panthers got the ball back and "Cam Newton" threw an interception.

Coach Wilson ran the ball again, and then went play-action pass for a touchdown. It was 14-0, and I could see Shawn was beginning to get frustrated—but also getting more determined.

Still, it didn't matter. Whatever Shawn tried to do, Coach Wilson would have the answer—and crush him. Shawn desperately tried to change personnel packages and attempted different formations and plays. Nothing worked.

In the end, after the score was 49-0 in the third quarter, they decided to stop the carnage. Shawn didn't have much to say, the trash talking had long since subsided, and Coach Wilson was too classy to kick Shawn while he was down. Coach did, though, throw in some zingers every now and again to remind Shawn of how cocky he had been.

It was kind of amazing. I had witnessed a late-fifties-something "old man" whip a teenage boy who could whip all his friends in . . . a video game.

Shawn simply said, "I don't understand what happened."

"You were playing a video game. I was playing real football," Coach answered.

"Well, I want to know how to do that too."

"That's what I am trying to teach you, son."

* * * * *

What we didn't know then was that Coach Wilson had been a consultant for EA Sports, producer of Madden NFL Football, to help them improve their game.

EA Sports had engaged many of the top-name college and NFL coaches to come in and discuss football and their plays and playbooks with their programmers so they could make the game more and more true to life. Coach told us that EA Sports had visited Pep Hamilton when he was the offensive coordinator at Stanford, and at the end of that visit Pep suggested they get in touch with . . . Steve Wilson.

Coach then spent time in Orlando with the game designers of Madden, befriending the programmers and staff. Coach told us one of things he had said to them was, "You all lied to me. Your slogan says, 'It's in the game,' but it's not." Everyone laughed, Coach said, but he also had their attention.

Coach proceeded to show them the nuances of defense and pass protections that were not in the game, and he challenged them to bring the game up to its billing! When Coach pointed out the finer points of the rules for Cover 3 "match," according to Coach the senior engineer said, "We can't do that; it's impossible." Coach said he replied, "No it's not. We can do it in real life, so you have to get the artificial intelligence to do the same thing."

And over the course of the next two years, some of those features started showing up in the game.

* * * * *

Coach Wilson told Shawn in one of his classes, "If you knew the code they used to write the program on defense, do you think that would help you in defeating the defense? Of course it would. Well, what I am teaching you is the code!"

It really isn't fair to play Coach Wilson in Madden. He is ranked in the top 100 players in the world, and he only does it once in a while so he can help the programmers continue to upgrade the game. I asked him how he got so good, and he said it wasn't his gaming skills, but rather his football knowledge. I don't think anyone can beat him in his football knowledge; therefore it would take a supreme gaming expert to defeat him in this football video game.

* * * * *

In 1993, Coach said, Pep Hamilton and Jay Walker and another of Coach's Howard quarterbacks, Ted White, were all experts in EAS Madden. "They would play each other and play me for hours during our quarterback meetings and after study halls. They thought they were just playing a game, but what they eventually realized was that they were learning some very important football as well. I had them install our entire offense in the game, so what they didn't realize was they were actually practicing for what they would see during the season."

Coach told me that he has always had a visual representation for the game of football. When he was young he first used bottle caps to represent the teams and then moved to the iconic electric football board game where he would line up the plastic figures for the national anthem and the coin toss and play not only entire games, but actually collect all the teams and play an entire season. Then in college, Coach began using the Madden game as a teaching tool for his teams. And now he was instrumental in changing the game, making it more real than ever before.

Coach said a little-known fact is that almost 20 NFL teams have at least parts of their playbooks installed on Madden, and they make it available to their quarterbacks for study and installation.

With Coach's help, the game is so realistic that the actual time frame the player has to snap the ball and throw to a target is the same 2.5 seconds that a quarterback has in real life in the NFL.

Coach asked me to try it, but the clicker still intimidates me. I told him that when they get voice commands, I'll be ready to "computer." And he answered that, well, the very next year they would have voice audible, so that all a player would have to do is say the play or the defense or the audible and the video will run the command.

I thought to myself: *This is like NASA simulator stuff.*

It dawned on me how fiction imitates real life and how real life imitates fiction. Coach spends his time trying to get the programmers to make the computer act like a human brain. And then he spends his time working with quarterbacks trying to make them think and act like a computer.

All I could think was: *Wow.*

Class 6

Key terms: *fire zone . . . tight third/loose third . . . heat 2 . . . Reno . . . seam flat . . . Tampa 2 defense*

Class 6 started with a review of the on-field session at Duke.

- "Great drills and speed and strength training, Shawn. This looks like college level to me." Coach talked about "popping the feet," and then loosening Shawn's shoulders and torso, being more relaxed, and carrying the ball with softer arms and with elbows down. "Allow the power to be generated naturally through rhythm, not brute force," Coach said. We looked at film of Andrew Luck [now All-Pro for the Colts] from his college career at Stanford, and Coach pointed out that "he is great with his feet, relaxed in the upper body, and has great rotation. You want everything to move in rhythm."

- Coach talked about how he asks his players to do pushups at the commercial breaks while watching TV. "I always have my quarterback do 'quarterback pushups.' The fists are together, and then go down slow and come up slow. Do five to eight with great form. Then hands flat and fingers pointed toward each other and the tips of fingers touching. Five to eight with great form. Then hands down by the hips, as far back as possible—do five to eight with great form. This strengthens different muscles and tendons around the shoulders and helps to generate power and protect from injury."

- After complimenting Shawn's throwing at the turf workout, Coach said the emphasis for a great quarterback should be to "throw with your feet. Remember, the feet are the engine and the motor. The ball has no energy source on board except what you put into it with your body. The arm is just the guide!" And he added, "Never let the ball out of your control, even after you throw it! . . . You need a good base with your hips and your feet because, remember: 'You can't shoot a cannon from a canoe!'"

Coach went on and had several compliments for Shawn, but it was also clear these kudos were wrapped in exhortations that Shawn needed to keep working . . . and working . . . and working, to become a better player, mentally, in every way, as well as working on his knee and body and overall strength.

Coach changed gears and began talking offensive philosophy.

- "Philosophically, everybody wants to go spread, spread, spread," Coach said, referring to the popular spread offenses that attempt to stretch the field wide and exploit the defenses with big gaps. "But look at Stanford and the 49ers and the Patriots. They are *adding* a tight end [an extra interior line player], or adding people to the core alignment. It doesn't even have to be a tight end per se. Compressing the defense creates another gap for the defense to have to deal with, or they are not sound. And when we compress the defense, more eyes are in the backfield, and thus more susceptible to play action, and that makes it harder for them to actually play the pass."

- "Remember, the goal is that there be no wasted plays. If we run sixty plays, likely twenty-five of them have the potential to be wasted because schematically they aren't great against a certain defense. But Shawn, the coach isn't at the line of scrimmage! If he were, he wouldn't call a wasted play. So that is the quarterback's job—*your* job! No wasted plays. Check to a good one, every time!"

- "Shawn, what I would like to start to hear is the dialogue that you have in your head as you see a defense: talk out loud so I can hear what you are thinking and what pictures you are seeing as you see them. Because, remember this: when the season starts, it's not what somebody else says to you, but rather what *you say to yourself,* that will make the biggest difference in your decision-making and performance."

Next, Coach was talking about controlling the pressure that comes from the defense so that the quarterback always sees it coming ahead of him, never from behind, never from his back, or blind side. "And you, the quarterback, are in charge of that," Coach said. "Call the protection and deploy the line and backs in a way that you can look right into the blitz and make the right read and throw!"

Coach explained that in practices he often ran entire sessions using "hot" protections; he would make the quarterback "fix it"—adjust what the offense needed to do—right at the line of scrimmage. "As quarterback, against blitzes, by the time you set your feet, you must already know where to go with the ball. As the offensive line coaches love to yell, 'Get it out!' Don't take the sack, get it out [make the throw], and make a big play when a defense tries to blitz you!"

Coach had a section on the famous "Tampa 2" defense as well. But it actually should more appropriately be called the "Steeler 2" defense, because it was first run to perfection by the 1970s Pittsburgh Steelers dynasty teams, of which coaching great, broadcaster, and Christian author Tony Dungy was a part, as a defensive back. When Dungy got into coaching, he took the defense to the Tampa Bay Buccaneers and advanced it even further as a progression-read defense that would morph into almost a matchup zone depending on how the receivers released from the line of scrimmage. It was more great football history being delivered from Coach to Shawn.

Shawn had a question: "What determines who is not blocked on a blitz?"

- Coach: "The quarterback does, by knowing the protection and deciding who you want to come free. For instance, say you use a base protection and have the running back check inside out on linebackers . . . Because the 'Mike' [middle linebacker] is the better player, we block him and leave the outside linebacker free. But now . . . think about this, Shawn. The defensive coordinator figures out your blocking scheme, and so he puts the Mike linebacker on the outside to beat the block of the smaller running back . . . Hmm. As quarterback, you see this, and you change to a 'slide protection' so that you get the Mike picked up and blocked by an offensive lineman."

- "Good offenses always change up their protections so the defense can't predict what they are in. Remember, every defense has a structural flaw—and so does every pass-blocking scheme, for that matter. Remember, you must protect against that, against your *own* structural flaws!"

- "A player can only process what his eyes can see and gather. So you have to be looking in the right place, and then you have to have enough stored pictures in your processor that, based on the limited information you gathered, you know what they can and can't do by knowing fronts and coverages you can anticipate, and you play faster than they can come, or faster than they can adjust. It's almost not fair! It's a little like running a 40-yard dash, but you get to take three steps before the starter says 'go.' And this is all because you have been running your processor mentally before anybody moves, and the ball is snapped, and you are already out of the blocks, under way, processing the play . . . seeing the play . . . way ahead of the defense. When you get to this point, it is almost like you now see in slow motion. You are never rushed, always calm. That is Joe Montana . . . Tom Brady . . . they almost snicker as they carve up defenses."

Shawn had another question. "Coach, but what if my high school doesn't teach this?"

- "Great question! The fact is that very few high schools teach this because the coaches don't know it themselves. But that's not their fault. They have three other jobs at school, they do the team's wash, have a family, and do the best they can. But here is the key: learn the principals of the protections, and learn how to protect yourself! As a quarterback, you must know what the line is trying to do and expect them to do it. And you must then work within that scheme to protect yourself in every situation. Your coach is teaching something, so learn it, and study it, and know where the issues are for you as a quarterback—and protect yourself."

- "For instance, Shawn, I really don't want to see you roll out the back door next year, like on your highlight film. You thought that was pretty nice, didn't you? Great. But Drew Brees and Brady and Peyton and Eli Manning don't have those plays on their highlights. And you know what? You shouldn't, either. So, know the protection, and if he [a blitzing defender] comes free, it should be in your face, the way you are looking . . . staring right at him . . . and then throw hot. Or, if you have to, juke him. But don't have him hit you in the back of the head, ever!"

Coach was ready to wrap it for this day. As he did, he went back to those basics, the most essential building blocks of all of this: learn the game the right way, put in the essential work now, on the front end, and the practices and season and recruiting and all the rest would take care of itself.

It sounded like a pretty good formula for life, too.

"Let's end here, Shawn, but let me say this. At every level of football I have been at—and your dad can attest to this—the more you learn, and it never fails, you always end up saying to yourself, *Man, if I had known then what I know now, I would have killed them back in junior high . . . or in high school . . . or in college.*

"So learn it all now, Shawn. And remember, there is only one game. Learn the game, and it applies at every level."

* * * * *

My arrival to each class would vary. Sometimes I would be waiting downstairs doing other work at my home office desk, at other times I'd be the last one down after I helped with the dinner dishes or helped give baths to the kids.

Eventually, for all of our sessions—which would number about 80 through the spring and summer and into Shawn's senior season—the three of us would assume our same positions in the basement. On one of the walls was a large whiteboard from Kate's second grade classroom from years ago; she brought the board home after she stopped teaching when she became pregnant with our triplets.

For most of our sessions, the board was covered with black and red erasable marker that showed Xs and Os and arrows and lines, the kind of stuff that most people recognize as coming from a football chalk talk session or a TV analyst's work. But the lines from the previous class were never erased, at least not until a new concept warranted that they be wiped away to make room for new learning.

And the learning that Shawn went through was amazing. Check that: the learning that both Shawn and I went through. There is no question that I soaked in all of this as much as Shawn, as much as I could absorb. I would need it for the challenges I was yet to face . . .

It was Football 101. Well, in truth, it was more like Football 701 or 801—advanced-level stuff. (We started at 101.)

Much more than football took place over those classes. Shawn's injury was healing, but more importantly . . . his mind-set was changing.

SEVEN

Class After Class

"Don't you ever tell me what is impossible"

Classes 10 through 22: May

Class 10

Key terms: *three-receiver hook . . . flat-foot read . . . curl post vs. post curl*

Coach was prepared to spend some time talking about the whole recruiting game.

"Shawn, regarding recruiting. Remember: it's marketing. So talking to the coaches from William and Mary and Richmond is great. They are good schools, and you also get to practice your marketing and make an impression on coaches who might end up somewhere else. And coaches talk to each other, especially now, before the January crunch time just before the signing date. And they compare notes on prospects, so a good impression on one goes a long way with others you don't even know about."

Coach had foreshadowed some key things for us in those few words: *an impression on coaches who might end up somewhere else.* Those words would be fairly prophetic in Shawn's journey. *And they compare notes on prospects, so a good impression . . .*

goes a long way . . . Unfortunately, just as true is his comment: "It's marketing."

But Coach had bigger things to focus on, so he kept working on Shawn's mind and overall game.

- "Shawn, we are identifying the ingredients to put in our cake. The first thing when you make any cake is to set those ingredients out on the counter, right? To make sure you have the entire recipe. The end process of the cake will not really show up with each ingredient as you work with them one by one."

- "When you can tear up high school defenses because of the *knowledge* in your head, it will be beautiful. At the end of the process, pictures show up in your head that you have never seen, but that you are *familiar with.* And you can process them fast, and then play faster than anyone else on the field. That's the goal."

And then Coach was off and running, playing with ingredients, getting Shawn to see how just the right footwork, or just the right read, or setting up the needed protection—how those things make the difference.

- "The protection is based on how many people we want into the route, and how many have free release with no blocking responsibility. The goal is for the quarterback and the offense to be ahead of the information, not behind it, or 'in it,' but *ahead of it,* so you can process it quickly and effectively—for success!"

- What Coach said next was critical. He pulled out the famous and ancient book, *The Art of War,* and began reading a section: "If you know your enemy and know yourself, you need not fear the result of 100 battles. If you know yourself but not your enemy, for every victory gained you will suffer defeat. And if you know neither your enemy or yourself, you will succumb in every battle." Coach was saying the same thing is true about knowing defenses!

- "Shawn, remember this. The defensive philosophy is going to be that every quarterback, even the great ones, are one player at the beginning of the game, and then they are somebody totally different after we hit them!" Coach mentioned some pretty good quarterbacks, very high draft picks, of the 1980s. "I remember playing against guys that were first round draft picks, and they were good in the first quarter, but after we hit them for a half . . . they were just ordinary. But not Elway, [Dan] Marino, and [Jim] Kelly. You hit them, and they still kept coming, making big-time plays. That's why they are Hall of Famers."

Coach closed this class with an assignment. "Shawn, I want you to tell us, next time, what are the dimensions of the football field, and what is the distance of the hash marks from the sidelines and the numbers and the middle of the field. Got that? Your assignment, son. Write that down. Take it seriously."

Class 12

Key terms: *spot drop . . . vertical hook . . . soft squat . . . kick and fade . . . middle of the half . . . China . . . zone it*

Coach jumped right in, picking up with the assignment from the previous class.

- "Here are some facts: The middle of the field is 26 1/2 yards from the sidelines. So if a safety in Cover 2 is supposed to split his half if he gets two 'verticals' [receivers heading straight upfield] attacking him, where should he be? Half of 26 1/2 yards, or thirteen and one-quarter yards from the sideline." Coach went on to get Shawn to think about the distance from the hash marks to the sidelines, and the top of the yard numbers to the sidelines, and where the safety would be in a slightly different alignment. He was getting down to precise, geometric stuff. But this was information that Shawn—or any attentive young quarterback, for that matter—could quickly process in his head to see where the safety should be, and what area should be open.

- "And if he [the safety] is not there, do you think that could be valuable to you as the quarterback to determine where to throw the ball? Of course! Big time!"

Class 14

Key terms: *pressure . . . clutch . . . leadership . . . the quarterback lifestyle*

Coach was talking about the famous play scripts that NFL teams use, in which they form a plan for the first fifteen offensive plays they will run. TV announcers talk about them like they are some sort of secret algorithm for success, but Coach was letting us in on the truth.

- "The play script was developed by Bill Walsh," Coach said, referring to the legendary San Francisco Hall of Fame head coach who innovated offenses in the 1980s while winning four Super Bowls in a dominating eight-year span. "But it was all for espionage. The first ten plays, they were all in different formations. They were all different plays designed to expose the defensive game plan against the offensive formations, against the offense's favorite plays, so that after the second or third series, the offense had a pretty good working knowledge of the defense's plan. We would then have our plan to defeat their plan. In other words, espionage, son! Few people understood this. They saw it as brilliant play calling designed to set up the offense for success from the start. It was designed to expose the defense."

Much later in the session, as usual, Coach was painting the big canvas for Shawn.

- "Let's talk about the 'clutch gene,' Shawn. What is it that separates the best quarterbacks from the rest? I call it being clutch. And over the years of being around and studying the some of the greatest quarterbacks of all time, I have come up with eight essential characteristics: courage, availability, consistency, driven, respected, inspiring, escape-ability, and being humble."

Then coach went to his UFU webpage and went through each

of these characteristics in great detail, using pictures and telling stories about all the great Hall of Fame quarterbacks he had been exposed to. I took notes as fast as I could. Shawn was transfixed.

Coach told two stories of his experience with a quarterback's leadership. "Coach Landry put me in the game as a wide receiver my rookie year with the Cowboys. I ran into the huddle, and when Staubach saw me, he said, 'Hey men, Stevie is in the game. Time for a big play.' I can't tell you how confident that made me feel. And sure enough, Roger threw me a deep 'in route' on that next play and I got my first NFL catch."

Coach continued in story-telling mode, this one from his first year as a Bronco with their new rookie, John Elway, at quarterback. "I had just gotten beaten for a touchdown and was kind of sulking on the bench. It was in the fourth quarter and I had put our team in a bad situation. John came over to me before the offense went out on the field and said, 'Hey, Stevo, I got your back on this one, no worries.' And he went out and engineered a touchdown drive to win the game."

Class 16

Key terms: *Cover 4-beater is 'PIG'—post and dig routes . . . BOSS: "backer over strong" . . . BOW: "backer over weak" . . . Rock 'n' Roll adjustment*

This class had a ton of very technical material. I was hoping Shawn was keeping up. I was trying to keep up.

Whoever said football is for big, dumb guys . . . they never sat in Coach Wilson's classes. It was like advanced calculus meets geometry meets physics meets psychology 851.

- "How do you ensure the comeback is open? You run the 'go' route often, Shawn, and throw it at 35 yards [downfield] so the defensive back does not have time to transition and pick up the ball. Most long balls are thrown too deep and become jump balls—all they do is show off strong arms. But the best '9' routes [a fly pattern, or the proverbial 'bomb,' where the wide receiver runs straight upfield] drop in at 35 to 37 yards deep, right over the outside shoulder, and the defensive back has little chance to make the play. Too many quarterbacks try to throw the ball too far and get into trouble, because at over 40 yards, the defensive back has time to find the ball and make a play."

- Coach always had stories, anecdotes from football fields all over America. Next up was this one: as a freshman at Alcorn State, Steve McNair (who would later become NFL All-Pro and take the Tennessee Titans to a narrow Super Bowl loss) would warm up throwing 20-yard boundary comebacks. Coach said he would watch warm-ups and see McNair throw the ball, then turn away . . . and talk to a coach . . . and never see the completion the receiver would make. McNair was throwing to a *spot*, not to a receiver. The throws were so on the money that he just *knew* they would be right there. "Lesson, Shawn: throw it to where the receiver *should* be, and over time, in the summer, in practice, he will get there!"

Coach had stories about the 1990s Dallas Cowboys, a team that won three Super Bowls in four years. Their defense ran Cover 4 so effectively that their offense had to come up with Cover 4-beaters in practice. They devised simple but effective offenses run by quarterback Troy Aikman, deep man Michael Irvin, tight end Jay Novacek, and running back Emmitt Smith running "Texas routes," in which Smith released and broke back across the middle of the field. That Cowboy team was rarely stopped.

Coach then went back in time for yet another story. Football fans know the Bill Walsh-Joe Montana glory years of the 49ers, and they know them well. Just before Jerry Rice became the best wideout of all time, on those San Francisco teams, Dwight Clark was an All-Pro wide receiver who helped the 49ers win their first conference title and thus first Super Bowl trip, which was a Super Bowl win (1982, vs. the Cincinnati Bengals). Cowboys cornerback Steve Wilson—Coach Wilson—was playing the boundary cornerback versus those 49ers during that first San Francisco Super Bowl season.

A young Steve Wilson actually could overhear a timeout conversation between Walsh, Montana, and one of the wide receivers. Steve heard Walsh say this to quarterback Montana: "Joe, let's just stay in the boundary and work this cornerback, who is high access, until he cramps? Then we will really work on his replacement in the second half."

Coach Wilson had a huge smile as he told this story. I don't know if he was expecting that Shawn and I would guess what came next, but he said, "I was already cramping at the time he said that! I wasn't able to break up the balls thrown due to their rhythm and timing. I recall making a lot of tackles that day, but I couldn't stop their completions. The 49ers were a machine that way." Coach had no problem telling a story on himself, especially if would help make his point in an even stronger way.

At one point, Shawn asked Coach, "What was the hardest you have ever been hit?"

Coach leaned back in his chair and said, "Oh wow, I'd have to think about that." And he paused. "I guess I have to say the 1986 AFC championship game in Denver. We were playing the Patriots, and I went in to make a tackle and I stuck my head into the running back's chest the way we were coached to back then, and at the same time one of my teammates was doing the same thing from the other side of the ball carrier. Our helmets collided, and that's all I remember about that game. I came off the field, they put smelling salt under my nose, I jerked my head back, tried to clear the cobwebs, and I got right back in on the next series. Man, for us, if you didn't play, you didn't get paid, so we all played through injury and hits to the head all the time. It was the only way you could stay in the league." And when one considers that Steve Wilson played a decade in the league and sustained many hits of that nature, or close to it . . . well, it's easy to wonder about the price that eventually is paid.

* * * * *

After class, Shawn had to leave quickly to do homework at his mom's, so I had the chance to drive Coach back home. We got to his place, but he couldn't find his keys to get inside, so we drove back to the house and, sure enough, they were sitting next to his basement classroom seat. We laughed about getting old and being forgetful, which was happening to me more often as well.

As we walked back to the car a second time, I asked him, "Coach, I have never seen you come into a session with an outline or syllabus for what you are going to cover." His answer blew me away.

"That's because my syllabus is entirely organic, meaning I read Shawn and I give him exactly what he needs each time. Sometimes he comes in distracted, not focused, probably doesn't even want to be there, and I have to engage him more. Other times he comes in cross with you because you have jumped him about his weight or his lifting or not finishing his meal or something and you two have a thing going that I have to work through. Other times he is high energy and ready to learn and locked in to what we went over last time and what is coming next. But the first thing I have to do is format him, like a new CD in the computer. It's not ready to record when you take it out of the package; you have to format it so the information you want to put on it will stick. That's what our first ten minutes of every class is about."

I wasn't sure I understood all that he had said, but I knew it was working and I knew every session was a new adventure with my 17-year-old son. So I asked him, "Is that why you tell so many stories?"

"Stories are the key to getting things into the student's memory," Coach said. "Most kids don't remember the details of what I am trying to teach, but they almost always remember the stories I tell. And that is why I use story; it is a memory device. It is the hook on which I put the information that I want him to have for the future, and the story I connect it with enables him to go and get it when he needs it, because he knows where it is in his mind. It is all filed by story."

I just said, "Wow, where did you come up with that?"

"Well, the truth is it is a technique that I have used for the past 25 years to help me with my memory and recall, and I have found it not only works for me, but it works for my players also."

By this time we had pulled back into Coach's driveway. He worked his way out of my hybrid SUV, not a car made for a big body like his, reached back into the car to shake my hand, and said, "Great session. Shawn is really coming along. Later." He grabbed his computer, projector, and briefcase and walked into his house as I pulled away.

Class 18

Key terms: *scat . . . 2-3 jet . . . full slide . . . max protection . . . flow*

Coach was set to go to work on Shawn again, to "format him" before the technical part of the football began.

"Shawn, regarding your injury: I know you are feeling great and all, but you are not ready to compete yet. It has been six months post-surgery, and the minimum is nine months before competition. So your first high school game will be cutting it aggressively.

"If you are not 100 percent, Shawn, don't run or compete. Scouts write what they see—without any explanation. I once heard an NFL scout say this, Shawn: 'You need to control how you are perceived, or how you're perceived will control you!'

"I coached dozens of players, over twenty years, who had ACLs. Some healed fast, some started over, some had trouble with the patellar graph . . . I had two guys want to play basketball too soon, and they ended up tearing the patellar tendon.

"Shawn, it's not ready for 100 percent until at least nine months—so hold the horses!

"After an injury like that, a lot of muscles stop firing, so they are learning to re-fire individually, and then will need to learn to re-fire as a groups. Shawn, that is still months away. Believe me when I tell you, it will take every minute up until kickoff that first Friday night.

"But the only thing that matters now is those Friday nights, Shawn. Everybody has seen your film. It speaks for itself. But they have to wait and see. They've got to see you compete under the lights. Against live bullets. They're asking: 'Will he be the same?'

"And the answer is, Shawn: *hell no!* You will be ten times better and stronger, and they will say, 'Wow, he doesn't look like 180 pounds; he looks more like 190. And that's not a 4.8 [40-yard dash] guy, that's more like a low-4.7 guy. And what great feet. And quick release. And what a processor—he gets the ball out to the right guy every time. Quick . . . wow! He is bigger, stronger, faster, and more efficient that he was!'

"Do your work, Shawn. Do it well, and diligently. With passion and urgency and commitment and focus and a little bit of an attitude . . . and it will all work out."

Coach told Shawn his next month would be about focusing on his footwork. And he had more on Brees: "Remember, Drew had a reconstruction of his shoulder, and nobody wanted him, everybody doubted him. And he was six feet tall and just 200 pounds. Do you think that made him burn? Gave him a chip on his shoulder? You bet it did!" And then Coach was taking the Brees example and making it personal for Shawn.

"How about you, Shawn? How will they tell the narrative about you looking back on the ACL injury in the playoffs your junior year? Did it break you or, ultimately, make you? It's your call, Shawn."

Coach said that quarterbacking had changed, was much faster, that more blitzers come free more often, and that the quarterback needed his feet always very low to the ground to be able to get the ball out extremely quickly and with great accuracy. Coach said that accuracy was ten times more important than arm strength, and then he told the story that has become folklore, when Bill Walsh supposedly told Montana to hit the receiver in the eye, and Montana asked, "Which eye?" Coach quickly said, "That's how accurate you need to be, Shawn.

"We want your mind to work at NFL-caliber speed, and your feet to work just as fast. If your mind can process at that speed, but your feet lag, you will not be effective. It's a waste. You've got to have them both working together.

"Most quarterbacks—no, almost all quarterbacks—come out

of high school and are ill-prepared for the next level. College coaches have to make a great investment in these players to teach them the nuances of the game. But if you can come in more prepared than the competition . . . you think that gives you an advantage, Shawn? Sure it does! That's what we are preparing you for."

Coach was then back on the mountain goat thing! "Those goats can climb a 10,000-foot mountain without looking down, almost vertical, straight up, and never look at their feet—and that goat's life depends on it! It's the same way with the quarterback. He can't look down at what is going on around his feet. He must feel it. He must react, relocate, escape, and make a play. All without looking at his feet! The quarterback's life depends on that ability too.

"Never thought you'd have to be like a mountain goat to be a great quarterback, did you, Shawn?"

Coach stayed in the animal kingdom with his next analogy. "National Geographic is a great channel. And it applies to football, Shawn! There are rules—really, laws—in the jungle. The lion eats when he is hungry, and the big fish eat the little fish, and there is a pecking order to all of life. But then there are hyenas. And they come in a pack, and they overwhelm the lion and frustrate him so they can steal his food. And that happens in football, too, Shawn."

Coach was talking about a sort of survival of the fittest, but also talking about the power of teamwork and how a group of hungry players, working together, can knock off a supposedly superior team.

'That's Impossible' (Class 20)

Key Terms: *under vs. over front . . . rotation . . . open vs. closed side . . . bandit . . . stack*

We were on field at the Duke lacrosse stadium and Shawn was going through some drills for Coach, who watched a few drops and throws carefully—he had been barking a few commands while doing so. And then he stopped, as though a light bulb had just snapped on.

"Oh, Shawn. I'm seeing something here. You are a three-repper. That means that it takes you three reps to pick up what the coach is trying to teach." Coach paused, as though thinking deeply. "Well, that's good, because it's better than most. But you know what, Shawn? It's not better than the two-repper; that makes the two-repper better than you. So, what do you want to be, Shawn? The quarterback who gets what the coach is teaching in one less rep than you—well, he is ahead of you. So then, your playing time and your career now depend on someone else and what *he* does. He has to screw up for you to get a chance. But you don't want to be behind him, Shawn. You want to be a two-repper. No, make that . . . you want to be a *one-repper*. So that when you get the chance, you take the ball and run.

"Remember, Shawn, a mental rep is the same as a physical rep. The body can't tell the difference.

"A good coach's goal is to make practice harder than the game! So, always go faster than you have to, Shawn, even as fast as you can, so that, in the game, things seem slower and easier. And . . . they are—even if you are playing Alabama. Or the Chicago Bears!"

What happened next stopped me where I stood. Coach had Shawn set up in the middle of the field for a drill in which he would chop his feet with the ball in what Coach calls the "ready balance" position. He then instructed Shawn to throw the ball to a slot receiver who was going to run downfield seven yards and break toward the sideline. But the key was he wanted Shawn to throw the ball when the receiver's hips dropped—before he made his cut. Sounded easy, and this obviously was designed to improve a quarterback's anticipation.

First rep: the receiver breaks out and Shawn throws a ball, the receiver catches it in stride, and he then turns up the field at about the numbers.

Coach yelled, "NO!"

I was filming from behind Shawn and looked up to see what the problem was. It seemed like a perfect ball to me.

"Do it again. This time earlier, Shawn."

Again, same drill, same outcome. Same shout—"No!"—from Coach.

This happened five times, and each time Coach was prodding Shawn to throw it earlier than he had.

Finally, after the fifth time, Shawn got aggravated from the criticism. "I can't throw it any earlier," he said to Coach.

"Yes you can."

"No, Coach. It's impossible."

"What?" Coach raised his palms. "What did you say?" He was looking at Shawn in disbelief.

Reluctantly, thinking he might have upset Coach, Shawn answered, "It's impossible. I can't throw it any earlier than that."

Coach jumped on Shawn. "Oh, OK. I see. So just because you haven't ever done it, or you haven't ever seen anybody do it, you think that is the definition of impossible? Well let me tell you something, son: you are wrong. I want you to throw the ball not when he makes his break, I want you to throw it the split-second his ass cheek begins to drop to indicate he is going to make his break. OK? Do it again."

They lined up again. Same drill. This time Shawn threw the ball so early I don't think the receiver had even started his break yet, but when he did, and came out of it, he turned around and the ball was literally hanging in the air right by his face, shoulder high. He snatched it out of the air and turned up the field on the hash mark. It was a thing of beauty.

Coach exploded. "There it is! *That's* what I am talking about!"

He looked at Shawn and said, "Don't you ever tell me what is impossible. Nothing is impossible if you know what you are doing!"

Shawn was smiling ear to ear. He had just done something he didn't think he could—and if that has ever happened to you, you know how exciting and fulfilling that moment is.

The next ten throws I recorded on film were perfect executions of what Coach was looking for. The timing was impeccable, earlier than even I had imagined possible.

Several times, throughout the rest of the classes, Coach would call on that moment and ask Shawn if he was saying something was impossible. Coach wasn't real big on *impossible*, and Shawn was careful never to make that statement again, at least not in the presence of Coach. It was quite a gift from teacher to student, one Shawn would never forget, and he would apply it many times in his future.

Class 21

Key terms: *match coverage . . . under call . . . 5 deep . . . 4 verts . . . seam flat*

Once again we were on a turf field in Durham.

Coach called this "assessment day, Shawn. We're going to see if you can make certain throws that no one can cover in high school, mainly because not many quarterbacks can make the throws, and then fewer coaches still know how to take advantage of a quarterback who can make them. So we are going to see what you got. And if you got it, great, we can go to work. But if you can't, that's OK too. We need to know it so we can build your skills around what you can do."

There were wide side 'sail' routes . . . wide side corner '7' routes . . . wide side 'go' or '9' routes . . . and a number more.

Shawn made all the throws, was sweating and breathing deeply, and Coach was ready to stop and discuss what he'd seen. He went on for several minutes, hitting a number of points.

"Shawn, you can make all the throws, big time. Now it's a matter of using the 'grown man' mechanics—but not just some of the time or even most of the time . . . *every* time you throw. . . . You need a great, wide base . . . fast, popping feet . . . great balance . . . great ball carriage, relaxed shoulders and torso, the appropriate shoulder tilt, depending on the throw needed.

"Now it's a matter of making every rep count, every read, all footwork. Every throw is college-level execution stuff. Johnny High School has got to go! That is what will make your offense unstoppable, no matter how your line performs, or how your running backs or your receivers or your defense does. You must play at such a level that no matter what happens, you are unstoppable! And you can do it. Not many can. You have the tools."

Later, Coach wrapped up this class with a final challenge for Shawn.

"Shawn, where you are, what you are doing, is about 80 percent correct. But the last 20 percent . . . the last 20 percent, Shawn . . . that's where the money is. That is the place to make you exceptional as a passer. That's where mastery is."

High School Coaching

During the summer, Coach Wilson and Shawn would look at Shawn's team 7-on-7 videos and Coach always had insightful and encouraging things to say. I was much more critical of Shawn, over and over, and I had a judgmental eye toward the coaching staff as well.

Coach Wilson pulled me aside one day. He asked me to meet him for lunch at the mall, which I did. He proceeded to scold me for, in essence, bad-mouthing the high school coaching staff. He told me I was often correct in my assessment of a situation, but that was not as relevant or important as it was to project to Shawn a confidence and acceptance of the authority and respect for Shawn's coaches. We owed Shawn that attitude so he could trust them during games, and vice versa, Coach told me.

I learned a lot in that exchange. And as I thought about it, I never heard Coach Wilson speak negatively about any other coach—period! Not Shawn's coaches, not coaches we evaluated on TV, in the NFL, in college, or other high school coaches. He just wouldn't do it.

I can be highly critical of coaches who show laziness or accept mediocrity in their teams or players. I'll voice those thoughts quite easily. But Coach brought me back. He's *forgotten* more football than many of these high school coaches have ever learned, but he doesn't ever trade on that. He remains graceful; he defers to the designated leaders of a team. What a role model that is for me.

Coach had a simple message. "Scott, you need to meet with the head coach man to man, if you have issues. Eye to eye. Sit across from him and tell him what you feel. But don't talk about him behind his back in front of your son. It is perfectly reasonable for you to meet with him and you set the agenda for Shawn's timetable and how his knee is doing. But you don't talk *about* your son's coaches—you talk to them."

That lesson for me served Shawn well too. Although I didn't actually end up holding to Coach's directive the entire season, I was much better than I would have been had I not been mentored by Coach.

Everybody needs someone to learn the hard stuff from.

Pressure (Class 22)

Key terms: *post corner . . . sail . . . stutter go . . . break high and quarterback throw-him-low*

"So, Shawn, your high school classes are over for the year. Lots of pressure off you, right? Summertime and no more responsibilities for grades and papers due."

Shawn smiled and nodded.

"So what is pressure? It's real, Shawn. It makes diamonds, and it explodes pipes, and it makes people react in right ways and wrong ways. It is real! It's a force from inside or outside that creates structural damage to its container.

"Look at LeBron [James]. In 2010, he scored, but he didn't win, and he didn't handle pressure well." (LeBron James spent his last year in his first stint with the NBA's Cleveland Cavaliers in the spring of 2010, and his team faded badly in the playoffs. The next four years, after changing cities and playing for the Miami Heat, he took his team to four straight NBA Finals, winning two of them.)

Coach went on with his LeBron lecture. "But boy, has he learned, huh Shawn? He eats up the pressure now. He thrives on it. He plays his best in the Game 6s and Game 7s, and in those 'gotta have it' moments.

"A coach needs his quarterback to want pressure, to revel in it, Shawn. To bite down and chew it up—that's a good thing.

"Under pressure, everybody else looks for a way out. But not you, Shawn. Not the best. You look for a way *in*! A way *through* it. When you can't change the outside environment that created it, you can change what's going on inside you. Everybody else reacts outwardly; you react inwardly. When everyone else says, 'We can't win. We're down two touchdowns' . . . or, 'We just can't block them' . . . that's when you say, 'Get me the ball. We can and we will—somehow!'"

Then Coach leaned back and asked Shawn, "Do you know the story of 'The Drive'?" Diehard football fans know that term refers to John Elway's classic touchdown drive against the Cleveland Browns in the playoffs. It's legendary stuff. Denver was at a frozen Cleveland Stadium, trailing the Cleveland Browns in the AFC title game with a Super Bowl berth on the line. It is January 1987. Elway's Broncos are down seven with two minutes left, and Cleveland has just punted Denver to its own 3-yard line. Ninety-seven yards away, 97 long yards from redemption.

Coach was on that team and described the offensive performance, which has become folklore: "John comes into the huddle. He has played OK, but not great for the entire game, and he says to the guys in the huddle, 'We got them right where we want them.' He proceeds to take us 97 yards for a game-tying touchdown, and we end up winning in overtime. Number 7 makes clutch throw after clutch throw with the game on the line. There was no pressure for him. He put everyone else at ease, and he led! That's what the great ones do, Shawn."

* * * * *

Coach switched gears from story to counseling. "Shawn, for the 7-on-7 passing competitions coming up at Duke this weekend and then ECU next weekend, listen to your body. Hydrate and work the fundamentals . . . keep a low, wide base. And have quick feet and don't hold the ball. We want to see you trying to do those things. But it's also your first time back under fire, so don't expect perfection. You will get fatigued and find yourself straightening up. You want to see yourself work under pressure, and remember: remind yourself to get your 'Drew Brees base.'

"And don't worry about the college coaches seeing you play. You are there on a business trip, and although it would feel good to be acknowledged by the coaches at Duke and ECU who will be there, remember, that is not your end goal. You are there to get better, to put good mechanics and decision-making on film, and to get ready for the season."

* * * * *

At the end of the summer, Shawn attended the one-day Vanderbilt camp for quarterbacks. The previous year he had done the same at Clemson and UNC, so he felt like he knew what to expect. This was a really important audition for prospective college players, when college coaches can work them hands on and up close to really get a feel for their talent and if they want to recruit these players or not.

Shawn and his mom drove out to Nashville and went to work, trying to get noticed by the Vanderbilt staff. He had a great day, throwing as well as any of the other quarterbacks that were there. He had a conversation with the Vanderbilt quarterbacks coach, and the recruiter for the North Carolina region introduced himself and said that he would be visiting Shawn at Cardinal Gibbons this fall.

Shawn was pumped. This was his number one school, and perhaps this would lead to a scholarship offer. But later the next week we read on the Internet that Vanderbilt had received verbal commitments from two other high school quarterbacks the same week Shawn was there. Shawn's heart slumped. So did mine.

Coach simply said, "Don't worry about it. It doesn't change the work you have to continue to do."

And he was right.

EIGHT

Why Am I So Tired All the Time?

"God hasn't abandoned us. I already checked with Him"

June, July

Shawn was in the full swing of football workouts and classes with Coach Wilson. Things couldn't have been going better in preparation for his senior season. I, on the other hand, found myself with an insatiable fatigue that seemed to be getting worse by the day.

It was a Wednesday morning on a bright, sunny day in July. It was July 17 to be exact, a day I will never forget.

The house phone rang as I was walking from the back room to the kitchen. The kids were watching a Nick Jr. show on the big-screen TV in the family room. The smart TV feature brought up the phone number and caller ID on the screen. It read "Duke Medical Center" and showed the time as 10:33 a.m.

My mind flashed back to three years earlier. We would see that caller ID often because our newborn babies were in the neonatal intensive care unit (NICU) at Duke. We had triplets born two months premature, and our daughter, Madison, died on her birthday, leaving her brother and sister to fight on. We baptized little Madison moments after she was born, and then she spent her entire life in our arms and on our chests in a private room throughout the day and into the evening of December 17.

Let me go back and fill in the gaps regarding my seven kids. Shawn's mom, Sue, and I married in 1986. We had Sarah in 1988 and Shelby in 1991. (Both are now married; Shelby married in 2015 and held her reception in the luxury box overlooking the football field at Kenan Stadium on campus in Chapel Hill—kind of poetic, and a thrill for an old quarterback like me.) Shawn was born in October 1995.

My divorce to Sue was finalized in 1998. I married Kate in June 2005. Three years after Kate and I married, my father, Leo, died of brain cancer. It was the next summer following my dad's death that Kate and I found out we were pregnant and expecting triplets! They were due February 17, 2010, the second anniversary of my father's passing.

Unfortunately, at 12 weeks into our pregnancy, we were told that Madison's amniotic sac had ruptured and that she was leaking amniotic fluid. Kate was immediately placed on bed rest and we were told to prepare for an infection to develop, which would most likely result in the loss of our pregnancy and all three babies. But just go ahead and try to tell a Stankavage what he or she can't do. Kate spent the next three months on bed rest (which was nice for the first day). After a few more complications, including two hospitalizations for pre-term labor, we got a call from our team of doctors saying it was time to deliver. There was more that they could do for the babies outside the womb at 30 weeks, versus inside, and it was getting too risky to keep them in the womb at that point. Ella Elizabeth was delivered first, at 3.1 pounds, then tiny Madison came next, at just 13 ounces. Lastly came Leo Dillon at 2.7 pounds; Leo was growth-restricted in the womb and was a big reason why we delivered at 30 weeks. Sarah and Shelby were able to come to the hospital to meet their sister Madison; Shawn wasn't allowed in because he was only 14 (hospital rules and regulations). Madison stayed with us for seven beautiful hours before she passed. What a gift for Kate and me.

We miss her deeply and think of her every day.

We visited the *twinlets*, as we call Leo and Ella, for the 86 days that it took for Ella, and the 126 days for Leo, to become healthy and strong enough to come home. Stankavages are fighters! Almost a year later, we baptized Leo and Ella at Duke Chapel on the Friday after Thanksgiving. It was that baptism weekend that we also found out we were once again pregnant! So we were now expecting Jordan to arrive just 19 months after the birth of the triplets. Oh my. You would never know that Leo and Ella had such a rough beginning to their lives, and Jordan keeps us all in line.

So, on that July 2013 morning, I was staring at the caller ID, remembering how that number was not typically associated with good news for us. Not once did the hospital call us to say, "Hey, Mr. and Mrs. Stankavage, we just wanted to tell you that your babies had a great night's sleep and their morning feeding went well and they are resting comfortably and waiting to see you when you get here!" That's just not how it ever went. And so, I braced myself on seeing the caller information.

I knew what the call was about; I was just uncertain as to what they were about to tell me. My primary care family doctor had spent the last five months doing tests and prescribing different medications to address my increasing sense of exhaustion and fatigue. We worked through the possibility of low testosterone and even depression and we examined my diet and added iron supplements. Kate and I were frustrated with the lack of answers, so we switched to a new general practitioner. My new doctor was young, and he wanted to find answers. This encouraged us. As a precaution, he decided to send me to hematology to run some tests to "rule some things out."

I had gotten in to hematology on a Monday and had a two-hour process of interviewing and questionnaires, and then they took blood from my arm, filling at least twenty tubes. "Wow, that's a lot of testing," I said to the doctor at the time, and she nodded and acknowledged, "Yes, we are going to be looking for some very specific markers to find out what is going on in your system."

And that was good. I wanted to know. Up to that point I had felt powerless in all my efforts to have more energy every day. It was hard mentally because, for almost a year, my energy had been declining, and I was getting frustrated not being able to reverse the trend with exercise or diet or sheer willpower. I had sensed something wasn't right when I had to lie down at the top of the steps before giving the kids a bath one night because I was out of breath. Knowing what was wrong, I was sure, would be a relief.

My brother Bruce had been calling to keep track of my blood tests; he wanted to help me find answers. We all knew that, conceivably, this could be cancer of the blood, or leukemia, or lymphoma. I had told Bruce we would be praying against these things as a diagnosis.

So as I stood in the living room that July morning, the phone rang a second time, and I looked across the kitchen at Kate, who had also looked up to see the caller ID. I muttered, "I will get it."

"Is Leo Scott Stankavage available? This is Dr. Silverman from Duke Hematology."

"Yes, this is he."

"Mr. Stankavage, we talked earlier this week when I did your blood tests. I don't have all the results back. But what I do have tells me that you have leukemia."

I swallowed. Probably a gulp.

"Hang on, doctor. I am going to put you on speakerphone so my wife can hear you, OK? Can you repeat that?"

"Mr. Stankavage, you have leukemia, and I have scheduled you for an appointment with oncology tomorrow morning at 10 a.m. It is important that you come in as soon as possible so we can begin to treat your disease because it is in an advanced stage."

Kate had tears streaming down her face. She had just lost her father, also to brain cancer, only four years after my father died, and two years after we lost Madison, and just one year prior to this phone call. This news was exceptionally hard for her to hear. I asked a few questions, and the doctor very politely and calmly finished our conversation by saying, "Mr. Stankavage, your situation is a complex one. There are more tests we need to run, and rather than give you a chemistry lesson in hematology and oncology, I recommend that you write your questions down for the doctor you will see tomorrow. He is a specialist in leukemia and is very good and considered one of the best in the country. He will be able to explain things in detail. I will not be treating you any longer, and I wish you the best in your treatment. OK? Good-bye, and good luck." And she hung up.

I hugged Kate. She cried. The kids were still mesmerized by the Nick Jr. show, which was fine with me at that moment. My overwhelming feeling was one of relief. I didn't feel scared or angry or afraid at all. All I could think was: *At last we know what is wrong. It hasn't all just been in my head. There is something chemically and physiologically wrong with me.* I wasn't just getting lazy since I turned 50, or, say, overwhelmed in helping my wife with our three young toddlers that we chased around the house. Relief was a big deal to me. Finally, we know. Now, instead of feeling helpless, I could develop a plan.

* * * * *

That same afternoon my mom called.

"Hi, Mom. How are you feeling? Do we have a plan for your chemo yet?" You see, my mom had been diagnosed with breast cancer the week before. Unbelievable, right?

"Yes, your sisters and I were at the oncologist this morning, and we decided that I would go through a three-month regimen of weekly radiation on my breast. The doctor thinks that we got all the malignancy out in last week's surgery, and he thinks this radiation protocol will kill any residual cancer that he didn't see. So I start on Monday, and just wanted to let you know."

"That's great news, Mom. Glad you got a plan, and it sounds like a good one."

"So, how is Kate and how are the kids? Everybody enjoying their summer?"

"Yep. Everyone is fine, Mom. Looking forward to going to the pool later on today and wearing them out for bedtime. Shawn leaves this Saturday for a retreat with his high school team as they begin camp for his senior year. He is pumped up about the season and can't wait to get started."

"OK, we will talk to you later. Love to all. Bye-bye."

And we ended the call.

I just felt there was no way I could ask her to bear the news of her oldest son's leukemia diagnosis knowing what she was going through with her own cancer. Wow. I had no idea how to handle this new information. Yet I had three older children, a brother, two sisters, and my mom, and they all deserved to know, and needed to know, what I had just found out. How was I going to tell them? And when?

* * * * *

My relief at knowing I was actually sick and not just lazy kept me from dealing with the actual diagnosis of Stage 4 (very possibly terminal) cancer in my bone marrow and blood. I didn't want to deal with it yet. And I didn't want to tell anyone until I had more details on the disease.

Kate and I met with the doctor the next day. I was officially diagnosed with CLL, chronic lymphocytic leukemia. It is a cancer of the bone marrow and the blood that is most commonly found in men past the age of 60. There is no cure. Ninety-eight percent of CLL cases are caused by a mutation in the 13th chromosome pair. It is often untreated, and the patient must manage the fatigue and exhaustion as best as possible. The typical life span is ten to fifteen years from diagnosis. The remaining 2 percent of CLL is caused by a mutation of the 17th chromosome pair. This is a more dangerous disease because it is more aggressive in taking over a person's bone marrow and crowding out the healthy red blood cells. This strain of CLL has historically been treated with cytotoxic chemotherapy, but that has met with limited success as it too often causes the cancer to mutate and become more aggressive. A bone marrow transplant is typically a last resort—a sort of Hail Mary treatment—as it carries many complications and only a 50 percent success rate.

The tests to determine which strain of CLL I had would require a bone marrow biopsy. This is a process where a nurse inserts a needle into the bone of your hip and draws marrow out into a tube that is then studied by the chemists in the laboratory. It sounds horrific, and I expected it to be painful, but with the medication I received and the expertise of the doctor, I only felt her tugging on my hip with all her strength to get the needle out. She said athletes tend to have very dense bones. I had proven this to be true.

We would have to wait a few days for the marrow biopsy results.

* * * * *

Later that week, I was in our master bedroom in the middle of the afternoon with a pastor friend, and we had my brother, Bruce, on the speakerphone, and we were offering up a prayer of healing. I had the door closed and my head was bowed listening to these men speak. Suddenly the door burst open; it was my three-year-old little boy, Leo. Once he had pushed the door aside, he marched right into the room without stopping and moved directly toward me, placing himself in a standing position between my legs. I was sitting in a leather chair with the phone on the floor. He put one hand on each of my knees and looked me squarely in the eyes; he has these piercing blue eyes. Then, with a little boy face, he said, "Daddy, are you sick?" as if demanding an honest answer.

There is no doubt in my mind that he already knew the answer.

Later that day, we were going out to eat as a family and I was strapping Leo's twin sister, Ella, into her car seat in our family SUV. Kate was on the other side of the vehicle and buckling in our youngest daughter, Jordan, in the middle, and then Leo off to her side. Ella blurted out, in the middle of being belted, "Daddy, I don't feel good. I have a pain in my bones. I can feel it all the way inside my bones. Something is wrong." I looked across the car at Kate, who was looking over at me. We held a glance for a moment and then shifted our attention back to buckling the kids.

I said, "Oh, Ella, where did you hear that? Something wrong in your bones?"

"I don't know, Daddy. That's just what I feel. Am I going to be OK?"

"Of course you are, Ella. Sometimes I feel that way too. But you are fine. Thanks for telling us how you feel. I love you, my girl."

"I love you too, Daddy. Can we get dessert after dinner at Tutti Fruiti?"

The beautiful mind of a three-year-old.

The incredible intuition of children.

Our children knew.

* * * * *

But Kate and I hadn't yet told anybody. I really wanted to know if I had the "17" or the "13 deletion." Kate and I would pray for 13, even though it's supposed to be an unlucky number. I am not superstitious, but I do like to be consistent with numbers. I associate the number 13 with two of the greatest quarterbacks of all time: Dan Marino (Dolphins) and Kurt Warner (Rams), who both wore jersey number 13 in their Hall of Fame careers. So I choose not to look at 13 as unlucky.

One morning, we had a doctor appointment with the oncology department at Duke. We met the first nurse and then another nurse and then a pharmacist and then a nutritionist. And eventually the doctor came and sat down with us. She started to talk protocol for CLL. We had been there for nearly four hours by this time! Nobody had told us what we were holding our breath about: was this cancer 13 or 17?

Finally I interrupted the doctor and said, "I have the 17P deletion, don't I?" I had read enough to know that the usual prognosis is that 17P is incurable, and that it carries a mortality rate of 24 to 36 months.

She looked at me and said, "Yes, you do. You have the 17P deletion."

Telling Shawn

Shawn was nearly ready for his senior season. He was undefeated as a starting quarterback in his high school career, and he was on the road, following his surgery, rehab, and classes with Coach, to being physically bigger, stronger, and mentally more prepared than he had ever been. He had a chip on his shoulder from being unable to attend and compete at the recruiting combines and was set to show the world that he was indeed a big-time quarterback, one that should be afforded his choice of where he wanted to play college football.

It was time for the season to begin. Everyone was excited.

* * * * *

So how was I going to tell Shawn that I had cancer?

Should I wait until after his team retreat? Should I tell him before? Should I do it over the phone, in a letter, or in person? Should I tell his coach?

I called Coach Wilson. I needed to let him know about my diagnosis.

"Oh my Lord, Scott. That's horrible. But listen, if there is anyone I know or have ever known who can beat this, it's you. So let me know whatever I can do for you. I'm here."

I asked him how I should tell Shawn.

Coach replied without a second of hesitation. "Man to man. Father to son. Look him in the eye and tell him the truth. And assure him he is going to be OK and that you are going to be OK. And tell him that the best thing he can do to help you in this fight is to go out and have the greatest senior year as a high school quarterback that anyone has ever seen in the state of North Carolina."

So that's what I did.

But first I called Shawn's head coach. I asked if I could come by the school Friday afternoon to meet with him face to face before the team left for the retreat. He was reluctant to agree to the visit because he had a "keep a good distance" policy with parents, and he probably expected me to have some opinion or advice about the program that he wasn't interested in hearing. I assured the coach that my visit was not football-related per se, but instead involved something personal with Shawn and his family that I thought he needed to know, especially given the retreat the team was about to take.

We met face to face, and to my surprise, I cried as I told him that I had been diagnosed with a rare type of leukemia—and that I had not yet told Shawn. I told the coach that it was my intention to have this talk with Shawn on Saturday morning before he came to school to get on the bus to leave for the retreat. I wanted him to know that Shawn would be burdened with this heavy information at the retreat, and I wanted to give the coach a heads-up in case he felt moved to pull Shawn off to the side and speak with him. And I said that if Shawn wanted to share this news with the team, it should be his choice.

The coach appreciated my contacting him and said he would approach Shawn in confidence and support him during the retreat and, of course, throughout the season. I told him that Shawn had shared with me that it meant a lot when the coach called him the night of his knee injury, before he went to sleep, and prayed with Shawn over the phone for healing and health, but also for God's will to be done no matter the MRI results the following day. So I felt great about the way this meeting went and about the coach's mentoring of my son in general. He is a spiritual man, and I told him that I believed his greatest asset as a head coach was that he kept the game of football in its proper perspective for his players. He was building a solid program and producing balanced young men who would be good citizens, husbands, and fathers for the rest of their lives. He could help Shawn put this in perspective and deal with it in a healthy way.

✶ ✶ ✶ ✶ ✶

Shawn was not scheduled to be at our house until the following weekend. Since he was two years old, Shawn had lived according to a custody visitation schedule that had determined, down to the minute, whether he was at his mom's house or his dad's house—every day of his life. It put a lot of pressure on him through the years.

I knew that asking him to break the predetermined schedule wasn't something he wanted to do. The most peaceful place he could be in his world was right where that schedule told him he was supposed to be. Anything different would upset his balance of life.

I had planned it out in my mind. I needed Shawn to get to our house Saturday morning at 8 a.m. before he had to be at the high school at 9 for the bus. I texted him; for teenagers, this seems to be the most reliable method of communication. He responded with: *I'm leaving for the retreat. I will see you after I get back.*

I pushed a little harder. He texted: *Why is it so important? Can't it wait til I get back?*

No, it can't was my reply text. That might have scared him, but I didn't know another way to require him to visit. It probably put him on alert.

Shawn said he would be at our house at 8 a.m. on Saturday.

* * * * *

I had spent the evening calling my oldest daughters, Sarah, 24, and Shelby, 21. After a game of phone tag with both of them, we finally connected and I told them about my diagnosis. One of the daughters handled it in a matter-of-fact fashion and was grateful for the call to tell her in person. The other daughter was in tears and concerned about what it all meant for the long term. I assured both of them that I was going to be OK and that I would keep them in the loop on news and information from the doctor with respect to treatment plans and any prognosis. I assured them that I would get answers to any questions they might have. I also asked them not to tell anyone else until I had a chance to tell Shawn the next morning.

Saturday morning, the toddlers were up early as usual. I had coffee ready at 6:30 and was done reading the paper by 7. Shawn showed up at 8 sharp; he seemed slightly annoyed and inconvenienced that he had to stop by before heading to school. He probably expected a sermon from me about leadership and the importance of his senior year and how proud I was of him and how hard he had worked and that now was the time to shine. Yada yada yada. That would have been par for the course from his dad.

Our little kids were already in full play. Kate said, "Hey Shawn, how are you this morning?" She tried to be as upbeat as possible and not foreshadow the news I was about to share. "Your dad wants to talk to you. Why don't you go sit on the porch outside where it's a bit more quiet and I will send him out."

Shawn went out back and sat at the picnic table on the deck. I came through the door and gave him a fist bump before I sat down next to him at the table. The kids were content, so Kate came outside and sat next to me at the table.

I could tell Shawn was slightly uncomfortable as he was sitting up unusually straight at the table as if preparing to receive a tongue-lashing or to have to stand up to some force that was going to come against him. I just waded in.

"So, Shawn, you know how I have been feeling exhausted and fatigued lately? Well, we had some blood work studies done at Duke this week, and we just got the results back yesterday. They said that I have a bone marrow and blood cancer, which is called leukemia."

Shawn looked me in the eyes as I spoke. He was expressionless. I wondered if he had already known, like Leo and Ella, or if he was just holding a stoic position because that was the best posture he knew to take to handle this news. Either way, he just looked at me, his chin held high and his eyes solemn; he kept looking at me without blinking. I was looking for some kind of read on his reaction, but there was none.

I continued. "We told your sisters Sarah and Shelby last night, and now you. I wanted my children to be the first to know and to hear it from me. And I thought long and hard about it, and I talked to Coach Wilson, and Kate and I decided that we wanted to tell you this morning before you went to Black Mountain and the retreat with your team. It's a heavy piece of information, and we thought it would be best for you to have to digest and deal with it while you were away."

Shawn nodded his head slightly, as if in agreement.

"I had a couple of blood transfusions yesterday and I feel great today. We have chemo scheduled to start on Monday that will use a targeted drug to hopefully knock out the cancer and put me into remission for a while. We have a good plan with the doctors at Duke, and I am going to be fine. If you think I am a tough son of a bitch as a dad and a coach, wait until you see me take on this cancer. Who do you think is going to win?"

I finally got him to smile.

"So that is what we wanted to tell you. OK? Do you have any questions?"

He merely shook his head. His silence indicated he was in full processing mode.

"OK, well I know you need to get going. Thanks for coming over, and sorry to hit you with such heavy news. But hey, this is life, and we are Stankavages, and we will get through it. It's not as though God has abandoned us. I have already checked with Him and He assured me He hasn't gone anywhere. He is walking with us every step of the way. So keep the faith. He has a plan and I trust Him for everything. Your job is to go and have a great weekend retreat. Lead your team and come back ready to kick ass your senior year. OK? Be safe. Get going."

Shawn walked back into the house, still quite stoic. He gave hugs and kisses to his younger siblings, and then I walked him to his car. We didn't say much. I hugged him and said, "I love you, dude." And he replied, "I love you, too."

As Shawn got into the car and started the engine, his radio blared country music. He quickly reached to turn it off, and then he looked at me through his open window. "Dad, they say God gives his most difficult assignments to his strongest warriors. Well, you are the strongest one I know. We will get through this." His voice broke up and trailed off.

"I know, son. You better believe we will!"

I waved as he backed out of the driveway. Shawn beeped twice as he shifted the car into drive. Then he disappeared behind the trees as he drove down the road toward his senior year of high school football, doing so with a repaired knee and carrying some heavy news. All of this was a much heavier burden than anyone expected he would be carrying.

NINE

First Treatment

"You are not going to deal with this alone.
We will all be with you"

July 22, 2013

Chemotherapy was scheduled for Monday at 7 a.m. at Duke Oncology. The Duke cancer center had been opened just months earlier, and it was as if the facility had that new home freshness and smell. It has a very gracious and open lobby, one that invites patients and families to meet with their doctors or receive their treatments, all in a warm setting. The environment is one of hope and peace. But there is still the reality of frail patients in wheelchairs being pushed across the marble floor wearing bandannas and hats to cover their bald heads.

Most patients seemed to be at the center with family. Chemotherapy consists of reclining in a chair or a bed for a few hours while poison is dripped into your system. It is not physically painful, but it is an emotional burden, especially for those under first-time treatments. It is an experience that most people do not go through alone. Lots of friends and family members wait in the lobby or sit vigil in the treatment rooms with patients. Cancer attacks families, not just individuals.

Kate and I drove up to the valet parking circle and exited the car, exchanged the keys for a ticket, and headed to the elevators. Those might seem like emotionally painful first steps for a Monday morning, but in truth, I was excited to have a plan. Ever since I was a boy, one of my favorite quotes growing up was, "Don't just stand there, do something!" Finally, I had something that I could do that would combat my condition. After all, athletes need a game plan.

The treatment was to be a three-month process that consisted of a cycle of steroids and chemotherapy administered intravenously every third week. The good news was that the doctors were going to use a "less toxic" form of chemo, one aimed at pushing back the cancer cells in my marrow and blood, and it was not expected that this would cause severe nausea, nor the usual loss of hair, nor a total depletion of the immune system. Remember, the traditional cytotoxic chemotherapies only "anger" this type of CLL, making it "smarter" and more difficult to treat. The doctors told us that this was a plan that would be adjusted on the fly after seeing how my body responded to the medicines. The hope was to keep the cancer cells at bay until the coming January (2014), when the FDA was expected to approve a new drug that had shown positive results in clinical trials for CLL patients.

Walking off the elevators onto the fifth floor, Kate and I turned the corner of the lobby and walked toward the reception and patient registration desk. After checking in, I scanned the lobby for a place to sit. An attractive blonde woman sitting in the corner at a table with a handsome, dark blond, athletic-looking man caught my eye. They both looked familiar, but truthfully, I didn't recognize them right away.

It seemed like thirty seconds, but maybe it was only two or three. I blinked and then it hit me: it was my oldest daughter, Sarah, and my younger brother, Bruce. I thought: *No, that can't be.* Both live in Charlotte, this was *early* Monday morning, and they would have to be at work.

As those few moments expanded, the young woman stood up

and smiled—a smile from deep in her heart. She began walking toward me with tears in her eyes.

"Hey, Daddy," Sarah said.

She wrapped her arms around me and gave me a big hug. For one of the few times in my life, this big, rugged ex-football player was without words. I just smiled as the tears welled up in my eyes.

I looked over at Bruce, who was grinning from ear to ear. We shook hands and hugged. I turned to Kate, who was standing in the background with a smile that just beamed.

"This was *you*," I told my wife with a bit of a choked voice. "You set this up!" Kate didn't need to nod. I knew.

"Dad, we just wanted to be here with you for this first chemo to let you know you are not going to deal with this alone," Sarah told me. "We will all be with you."

I turned to Kate and hugged her. I whispered in her ear, "Thank you, sweetheart."

* * * * *

Coach Wilson was there for me also. He helped me see that facing leukemia was like facing the blitz: meet it head on, be confident in your plan, and then execute. Given the possible alternative outcomes with CLL 17P, I was facing the meaning of life and leaving my legacy. Hard things to think about, Coach said, but necessary ones.

Coach told me a story that when he was younger he was absolutely terrified of graveyards. One day his grandfather took him for a ride to the church and made him walk through the graveyard with him. The old man and his grandson stopped at one of the headstones and his grandfather said, "You know what the most important part of your life is?" A young Steve shrugged his shoulders. The older man said, "The dash"—and he just pointed to the small line cut into the stone between the four numbers on either side. "The most important thing about your life isn't the year you were born or the year you died. It's what you did in the dash."

Coach said to me, in a private talk, "You are making the lives of those you are responsible for better, easier. You are setting the table, Scott. You are holding onto a dream and a future—for others, your family—until they can see it and hold it for themselves. That's what great men do. You are making the most out of your dash."

I guess a diagnosis like this gives you a huge dose of perspective. Problems you thought you had shrink to nearly nothing, and life develops a huge urgency. *I will beat this thing* becomes a common mantra. And then there are also countering thoughts: *What if my time is more limited because of all this?* Regardless of where my thoughts take me, I am even more resolute in my priorities and know exactly where they should be. My faith, and my family.

Obviously, I took my diagnosis extremely seriously and part of that was to make a plan for the worst, for not being here in a few years. Kate wasn't always happy to discuss such matters, but I felt like it would be irresponsible to not have a plan in place to make sure everyone was cared for to the best of my ability. But after a month or so of that focus, I ended up realizing it is equally as irresponsible to not plan on living, that I should plan on the prayer and medicine beating this disease that to date was incurable. I reflected on how Coach was talking to Shawn about overcoming huge odds stacked against him and that Shawn should plan on things that he could not see and that others didn't believe possible. And then I realized that, well, I had to do the same thing.

Coach's classes with Shawn and me were far from over. Secretly, I couldn't wait for the next ones. I had my own battles to beat. I was excited for Shawn and I to get back to work with Coach.

TEN

Father and Son

*"It's time to stop pushing your dad away
and let him father you"*

Late Summer

Classes during those initial weeks of the preseason of Shawn's senior year were focused on the art of quarterbacking instead of the technical elements of defense or alignment or strategy; we had gone over many of those things in the early and late spring. At this point, in August, Coach would spend time asking Shawn how he handled the huddle, how he addressed receivers who dropped passes, or how he handled himself when the coaches were critical of his decision-making or his execution. Coach asked Shawn to tell him about conditioning and if he would come in first in the sprints or if he would lag behind.

When Shawn told him he was always first or second, Coach asked him what he did once he crossed the line. Coach said that after finishing his sprint, Shawn had a simple job: turn and encourage every last teammate as they came across that line.

* * * * *

Coach arrived early one night before our scheduled class and went downstairs and set up Madden. When Shawn and I headed down, he was already on the screen playing.

He said, "Sit down. We are going to see how much you've learned."

And the two of them played head to head for the next 45 minutes.

The score at the game's half was 28-21, Shawn winning. And he was grinning ear to ear. Coach said, "OK, that's enough. You have come a long way and I can see you applying the lessons from the class to the video game. There is a lot more to learn, but this is the greatest simulator for quarterbacks that I have come across." And they stopped the game at that point and Coach pulled up the Ultimate Football University website, and the next class began with some film of Tom Brady. The reality was that the class had actually started with the Madden game, and Coach was using that platform to show Shawn how far he had come in his learning of the science of football. It was a sneaky way of saying to Shawn "nice job" and growing Shawn's confidence in his skills.

* * * * *

Coach called me one morning, and when I answered I heard, "Hey Scott, what did you do to Shawn? He called me last night all shook up. He canceled our session at the last minute to take his girl to dinner, and he said you were all over him and called him out about his passion and his commitment."

I shifted in my chair. I was guilty as charged on the count of rebuking Shawn for canceling class at the last minute, and I may have gone a little overboard with my scolding, which would not have been unusual for this dad.

Coach paused, but for only a quick beat.

"But hey, that's not a bad thing. He needs that. His plate is full and he doesn't know how to manage it this full, both mentally and physically, and this is his first time managing a girlfriend. And we know that is an art in itself, especially for an athlete. And if you went off on him, well, that's OK too. It won't be the last time someone gets on his ass and questions his commitment and focus or calls him out. He needs to know how to respond to that before it happens in college. He won't be able to quit or run away there. He will have to man up and own his decisions. And he won't be missing or skipping or rescheduling any coaches meetings in college—that is guaranteed.

"Truth of the matter is, you are fathering him, and you have mostly been his buddy, but now you lay some heavy fathering on him and he doesn't like it. He isn't supposed to. So he runs away to his girlfriend. Fact is, he has to stay in dialogue with you, and I know you haven't bad-mouthed his girl or his friends. He just doesn't know how to say no or prioritize. Truth is, he can have all his friends, but after he gets his work done. And he must have a priority that he can't last-minute change the schedule for class or workout because his girl or his buddy wants to go out to dinner or go fishing.

"Remember, Shawn usually responds big-time when you challenge him, so that is what I expect from him this time. Let's see how he does. But don't back off. You did a good thing for him; he probably needed it.

"So good job, Dad. And we will see you tonight."

There was a subtle message underneath it all, one that had at least two sides. You're his dad, so father him. But there was also a hint of this: Remember, he's still a very young man trying to find his way and his place in the world. Never forget that, either, Coach was saying. Shawn needed balance from his dad.

* * * * *

Several weeks later, we had finished class in the basement, right at about the 90-minute mark, and like clockwork, Shawn's attention span had run out. So when Coach said, "Let's stop here for the day," Shawn closed his notebook, got up from his chair, and reached toward Coach Wilson to give him a handshake. It wasn't a formal business handshake, but the less formal one often exchanged between athletes, and Coach nodded at me; he had recognized something. He closed up his computer and wrapped the cords neatly, as he always did, then headed up the steps.

Nothing unusual about the end to this class.

Coach and I headed outside. After some small chatter about when our next golf game might be, Coach mentioned how he thought Shawn was really picking up the information and that he could sense his growing understanding of the big picture. Teachers enjoy it greatly when they see their students learn, and I could sense that satisfaction in Coach Wilson.

We talked for a bit longer in the warm sun. Coach had his EA SPORTS baseball cap and Howard University football shirt on, his computer slung over his shoulder. And then the conversation suddenly turned quite serious. Coach had driven home with Shawn following a session a few nights earlier, and he wanted to talk about that conversation.

Coach started, "So, I really laid into Shawn the other day."

"Oh yeah? What happened?"

"Well, I've been watching Shawn now for some time, and I can really relate to his family life given the divorce and the conflict between mom and dad. And I have been trying different things to get him to respond differently, but they haven't seemed to work to get him where he needs to be. So I was talking to my wife the other night, and she listened to me and then said something very profound. She said, 'Steve, you are trying to do it *for* him, when what you need to do is just come out and *tell* him.'"

I was intrigued, quite curious as to where Coach was going with this.

"So the other day, in our time with just me and him, I just told him," Coach said.

I didn't say anything, but just raised an eyebrow, and I was sure Coach read me. The expression said: *OK, what did you tell him?!?*

"I told him, 'Shawn, you need to let your dad father you.'"

"Whoa," I said. "What did Shawn say to that?"

Coach replied, "He got a little defensive, which I expected. But I told him this was one of those times where he was just supposed to listen and not respond. And so he did.

"I told him that, from what I could see, he had been raised in two loving households that had both similarities and differences.

And the majority of his time was spent in his mom's house with his two older sisters, who loved him very much. And women have a way of nurturing and supporting that is different from men. And I told Shawn, 'Your dad has been cast as this big, bad gorilla that just pushes you too hard or demands too much of you.

"'I've been watching this, Shawn. And so, you have developed a way of just tuning him out, or waiting him out 'til your time with him is done, and then you hightail it out of his driveway as fast as you can. I've seen this time and time again.

"'But here is the reality that you will have to eventually face, Shawn: It is not up to your mother or your sisters or your girlfriends to show you how to be a man. I see your dad trying to father you. He wants to teach you what he knows about being a man. And you shut him out. You let him be your friend. You let him buy you things and provide all the best things for your career and your recreation, but when it gets down to the hard fathering moments, you shut him down and run away.'"

Coach wasn't done. Now came the deep stuff. "'You can't do that anymore, Shawn, because you gotta learn what your dad has to offer you. It's like those scrapbooks of his. You think there are any lessons in there that could apply to your career? He led the country in passing for most of his senior year in college, ahead of NFL players like Steve Young and Boomer Esiason. He knows things, Shawn, that only he can teach you. And you need them. It is what a good father gives to his son. And you are refusing to let him father you.

"'And now, with his leukemia and his unknown future, Shawn, he has an urgency about him and his life that has turned up his awareness of those things that he wants to give you. But still you push back and call him over-the-top. The reality, Shawn, is that he isn't over-the-top. And if you think he is, you will never make it to where you think you are trying to go, because in that place, where your dreams are, over-the-top is a part of everybody there.'"

"So I had Shawn's attention, Scott, but probably not his agreement," Coach told me. "So I hit him with the whole truth.

"I asked him, 'Shawn, if something happens to your dad with this leukemia that he has, let me ask you something. Who is going to show your little three-year-old brother Leo how to be a man? Who is going to teach Leo all the things that your dad would have taught him?'"

And that choked Shawn up, Coach told me; Shawn had been visibly upset. I have no doubt that Coach was gentle in his tone, but he had a strong message to deliver and he wanted Shawn to deeply understand what he was trying to convey. And then Coach took me back to the moment between him and Shawn.

"'Hey, it's no time to cry about it, Shawn. It's time to do something about it. It's time to stop pushing your dad away and instead, let him father you. That's all. It's his job, and he takes it very, very seriously. So stop running away to places where you aren't held as accountable for your actions and your dreams. Where saying 'I tried my best' is good enough—even if it's not.'

"And Scott, ever since that conversation, I have seen a different Shawn coming to our classes. He sits up, he listens, he takes notes, he asks questions. He is slower to leave after class and he has conversations about things other than football. I know he heard me—and he is trying."

I'm not sure anyone else could have conveyed that message to Shawn in such a graceful, yet impactful, manner. I felt blessed to have Coach in our lives. I have known some men who would resist another man "fathering" their son so directly, but not me. I count it as a blessing. I believe masculinity is bestowed, and I believe it comes through the words of another man. Ideally it is a father, but it doesn't have to be. And in Shawn's case, Coach was addressing things that I didn't have the ability to convey to my son. Like so many other 17-year-old boys, they won't listen to their dad, but if another father or a coach tells them the same piece of advice, it's like gold. So for me, I was so thankful for the relationship Coach had assumed—and accomplished—in Shawn's life. It meant a lot to all of us.

We got in the car to drive Coach home, and I inquired deeper about his philosophy in working with young men.

He said, "Often players will come to me with a mind-set that they are primarily and solely an athlete. They seem to be out of touch with the fact that they are also a man. And they certainly don't get that the being-a-man part comes first and foremost. They are a man who also happens to have athletic talent. Just because they have been called an athlete their whole life, that doesn't mean that is who they are. The man and the athlete are two separate things. And almost every player I address will argue with me when they are younger, and they will tell me, 'No, Coach, I am an athlete. That is who I am.'

"So I explain some things: 'If the athlete gets hurt, then who are you?' And they can't answer that question. It is the inherent problem in a lot of young people today. Their entire identity is tied to their athletic success, and once that is gone, whether it is taken by injury or competition or old age, they are lost for an identity as a man.

"I don't want that for any of my players. Because when football is over, I want the man to lead a successful and meaningful life as a husband and father and member of a community."

I reflected back to Shawn's poor decisions after his ACL surgery. The beer party and his flipped car. Shawn's identity was so wrapped up in being an athlete. When that was taken away from him, he was lost. He was a prime case in point of what Coach was referring to, and I was glad to hear Coach's philosophy, as it affirmed my own. First and foremost: you are a man, a man who also happens to be an athlete. I wanted Shawn to understand this deep in his core, and I was certain he was on course to do so.

Before Coach got out of the car, he turned to me with one last nugget of wisdom: "You can't make Shawn do or be anything, Scott. The fire from within has to come out. We can set the table, but ultimately it's up to the man, and the athlete within the man.

"So it's time for you to back off a little, Dad. We poured the concrete on this one already, and it's time to let it set. OK?"

That got my attention.

ELEVEN

Back to Football

"No setbacks!"

Fall, Shawn's Senior Year

As the preseason football camp got started for Shawn and his teammates, news of the leukemia had gotten out. Some of the parents of boys on the team reached out to me to express sympathy and offer prayers. Shawn had shared the news with the team, and everyone was fully supportive of him and our family. We were grateful for the extra support, especially for Shawn. The ACL tear, surgery, and recovery (both physically and mentally) had been a long, hard process. Shawn no doubt felt extra pressure about being under-recruited. I had no way of knowing how heavy a burden my diagnosis was for our son. And lastly, this year's team had lost many key seniors from Shawn's junior season, when the team went undefeated with Shawn as quarterback.

I went to the first official practice of the year. As could be expected, the defense looked dominant on the first day. And the offense looked crisp in drills. It seemed that everyone was on the same page. One of the other parents came up to me and asked, "How do you think we will be this season?" I gave a simple answer: "Fine."

"I think we will be lucky to win five games," he said.

I didn't say much. That's not what Shawn, Coach, and I had in mind, but I kept my thoughts to myself.

* * * * *

Cardinal Gibbons' first scrimmage was on a Friday afternoon in Raleigh against regional powerhouse Wake Forest Rolesville. I had a three-hour chemotherapy infusion that morning, and I was really dragging. But there was no way I was going to miss Shawn's first tackle football event since last November. It was a long drive for me, slumped in the passenger seat, as a friend drove us to Raleigh for the game. It was a long walk from the parking lot to the stands, and it felt like I was moving at a snail's pace, stopping to catch my breath every five or six steps. Not fun. But I was going to get there eventually, that was for certain.

As I walked into the stands, I waved to a number of parents. I am not a very social parent when my kids are playing. I prefer to sit by myself and view the game, the coaching, and everyone's play, and truthfully, I do it in a less-than-social way. If I'm honest, it's the residual burden of having played the game at the highest level; the training never leaves you, and it's hard to just watch any game as a spectator and enjoy the game for the game itself. My mind has been trained to always read coverages and anticipate defenses and play calls and coaching strategies. I wish I could turn it off, but over the years I've quit trying and have accepted that this is just the way it is, the way I'm going to experience sporting events, especially football.

For this first big stretch of live action (no longer only 7-on-7 drills), Shawn wore a knee brace. It was his first football under fire since surgery just eight and a half months earlier, and while the leg was actually stronger than it was before he was injured, no one ever quite knows how an athlete's mind will recover.

As the scrimmage unfolded, Shawn looked strong and threw with confidence. I could tell he was tentative at first, and it actually took a couple of collapsed pockets to force him to scramble around and knock the cobwebs off, to force him back to his instincts and the flow of his natural skills.

The next day Coach watched the video of the scrimmage with Shawn and was extremely pleased with what he saw. He was highly complimentary of Shawn's footwork and recognized his instincts to move around in the pocket and scramble, even though he didn't yet have the balance and speed to be as elusive as he once was.

Overall, Coach said, it was a great start.

Lessons in Mortality

The next week, I decided I would drive over to the high school and watch the last part of practice on a Monday. The drills were crisp and the coaches were encouraging.

As practice came to an end, the coach called all the boys up for final comments, announcements, and what is usually some encouragement about staying hydrated and getting a good night's rest. Whatever was said, the boys were glued to their head coach; the mood somehow seemed different. I left to beat the traffic and head home.

It was a Monday night, so per the visitation schedule, Shawn came to our house after practice. Kate made spaghetti and I had waited to eat with Shawn when he would arrive at 7:30. Kate was upstairs negotiating bedtime with the three little ones, so it was just Shawn and I sitting at the dinner table.

He asked me, "Dad, did you know Will's dad, Mr. Graham?"

I told him that, yes, I did, from some work in real estate, and Mr. Graham had supported the Durham Eagles Pop Warner football organization. I had just talked with him two weeks earlier at a practice in which Mr. Graham had asked my opinion of whether his son should spend the season on JV—where he would play, and play lots—or watch from the sidelines as a sophomore on varsity. (My advice had been to have his son play JV; nothing beats actual playing time versus just standing and watching.)

Without looking up, with his fork twirling around in his spaghetti bowl, Shawn said, "Coach told us after practice today that

Mr. Graham died of a heart attack earlier this morning."

I gulped, dropped my fork, and put my head down. *Oh my Lord* was all I could think.

Silence.

"How are you doing, Shawn?"

"I can't believe it for Will. I can't imagine that happening."

Shawn didn't tell me about his tears as the head coach broke the news to the team; the coach told me later that he saw Shawn on one knee with tears streaming down his cheeks. The news hit close to home; it was a jolt into that place in his heart where he closely held his own father's mortality while dealing with my Stage 4 leukemia.

Shawn and I spent the next five minutes in silence, eating. I didn't know what to say. I wanted to say something, something comforting and profound. But silence was my best effort; it seemed better than saying something trite or inappropriate or corny. My son and I sat together, feeling the weight of a team-mate having lost his father that morning. Feeling the weight of the future and its unknown outcomes associated with my diagnosis. It was heavy.

That weekend, on a Sunday afternoon, all the boys on the team attended the funeral in Durham for Bill Graham. Bill was a gregarious, smiling, joyful man of God. He was always spreading encouragement and optimism whether he knew you or not. The funeral was a testament to his life. The team walked through the line to offer condolences to Will and his mom and sister.

During the eulogy, which was a wonderful testament to Bill's positive attitude and living life to the fullest, Shawn came to the back of the church and sat next to me.

We didn't say anything. We were just together. That was enough.

* * * * *

Coach and Shawn were scheduled for a class the next week at 7 p.m. I was ready at 7, and I could see Shawn's car in the driveway with Coach in the passenger seat. It was an hour and a half before they came into the house. The mood was somber as they moved down the steps to the basement. We had an abbreviated session that night, watching some film of Tom Brady and Peyton Manning. I went upstairs before they finished, saying good-night at about 9.

The next morning Coach called to tell me what had happened. "Sorry we were late for last night's session, but we had one going on in the car in the driveway. And it was an important one. I asked Shawn how hearing of Mr. Graham's death affected him, and he opened up a little. So I reciprocated. I took the time to tell him about when I lost my dad and how hard that was for me. I also told him about when I lost my younger brother to cancer a year earlier. Man, those were some dark days for me, and I shared some of my grief with Shawn. We connected last night. That's all I can tell you, because the rest is between me and him, but I just wanted to let you know he is processing it all as best he can. And I also want you to know he is a strong young man with a big heart. You should be proud of him, and I am proud of the job you have done in raising him."

I was humbled, and grateful.

* * * * *

The team next scrimmaged Garner High that Saturday in the Pigskin Preview. Garner was another state powerhouse and recent state champion. On paper it would seem to be no match between the Gibbons private school 3A program and the dominant Garner Bulldogs. But, playing in a soft drizzle, it seemed as if Shawn announced that he was going to be a force to be reckoned with no matter who the opponent was. Garner played a zone defense on the first two possessions, and Shawn completed 8 of 9 passes for two touchdowns. Lots of people were caught by surprise by how well Shawn and the Gibbons offense played. Garner then decided to make some major changes on defense, and the Gibbons offense struggled from then on.

As usual, Coach was all over it; it came out in the next class, the very next night in our basement.

Coach Wilson put on the video of the Garner scrimmage.

He was complimentary of Shawn's fundamental footwork, ball carriage, and anticipation of his throws, especially against the zone defense. But before the third series, coach stopped the film abruptly and asked Shawn, "So, if you are the Garner defensive coordinator and you just got carved up by the quarterback on those first two drives, what are going to do?" Shawn said, "Change up the coverage, go to press man, and see if the offense can handle that." Coach: "And that is exactly what happened." We went through the rest of the film and concluded there was a lot of work to be done to prepare as a quarterback to deal with press man defense.

Coach stopped the film session and went back to some of the sessions we had been through earlier in the summer that dealt with man-to-man coverage concepts. He reminded Shawn and reviewed with him the idea that against man-to-man defense there is no progression for the quarterback; rather, he must select his best matchup and throw away from leverage. "Pick 'n Stick" is what Coach called it. It all made sense and would be necessary for Shawn and the offense to be successful later in the year. It was a great learning session.

* * * * *

The regular season started against a larger school, 4A Green Hope. It was late August, a perfect night for summer football. A 95-degree afternoon had cooled off just a bit, so it wasn't quite a sauna for the players, but it was hot. Breaking a sweat in warm-ups wasn't an issue; in fact, players broke out in a decent sweat just putting their pads on.

The pageantry was terrific as the seniors carried the school's symbolic sledgehammer in front of the team as they walked two by two through the bleachers and onto the field for the national anthem. Gibbons was in its home all-black uniforms.

Shawn took the field and immediately took control of the game with short, crisp passes. Then, when the defense had been drawn up, he dropped back and faked a quick slant. The wide receiver, one of Shawn's best friends, Dante DiMaggio, turned upfield, caught a fade route, and raced into the end zone for a 74-yard touchdown. Later in the second quarter, Shawn carried the ball and had his helmet come off, so he had to come out for a play. His backup quarterback, DiMaggio—who, by the way, is great-grandson of Yankees great Joe DiMaggio—went in for one play and threw a touchdown pass of 35 yards. The score was 14-0 at half.

Green Hope made terrific adjustments at halftime, though, and kept Gibbons from scoring the rest of the game. Green Hope easily could have won. It reached the Gibbons three-yard line by the game's final play, and sent in the field goal kicker. The boy missed the short kick, however, and Gibbons had a win. Shawn finished 11 for 27 for 177 yards, two interceptions, and the one score, but these were not statistics that warrant a college recruiter's attention. Hardly his best effort, but Shawn had won his thirteenth straight start as a high school quarterback.

* * * * *

So it was back to practice to prepare for the next game. Coach had always emphasized the sanctity of practice. I had written—dozens of times in my class notes—Coach's statement that to play fast in the games, you have to practice fast. And Coach always preached that practice was the place to become a dominant player in every drill, in every period, and on every rep.

So in the next class, we went over the Green Hope film. One of the realities I've discovered as an athlete is that film is an interesting animal: you never look as good as you think you did, but also, the opposite is just as true. Even when you think you've played horribly, it doesn't look as egregious on film as it felt on the field. And that was true of Shawn's first game back.

Shawn had some struggles in the Green Hope game, but Coach stayed almost entirely positive. "Great work! You are playing live football nine months after a full ACL knee reconstruction!" Coach stressed how unlikely it was that Shawn would be playing at such a high level again so quickly. He helped both Shawn and me to lower our expectations and realize that what we want to see is improvement from week to week, not perfection.

And Coach reiterated the mantra of David Roskin: No setbacks! David was emphatic about that with Shawn, not wanting his recovery to face any setbacks or even time off due to soreness or re-injury.

I have used that piece of advice a dozen times to other athletes and parents since Shawn's surgery. It is the best advice I've ever heard, and it incorporates so many things: *No setbacks*. Maybe you're dealing with Stage 4 cancer, or a financial burden, or struggles in parenting a child. Doesn't matter. To me, *no setbacks* simply means that you keep moving forward.

As we continued watching the game film, Coach started in on a new subject. "Shawn, here is the problem. It's a chess match out there, not a track meet. You have an arithmetic problem in front of you. They have seven guys in the box: angry, stronger, bigger, and faster athletes about to try to come and decapitate you. And you only have six bodies to defend your skinny little butt. Uh oh. Which one of those guys is going to come free? Do you know?

"You don't. *You* better figure it out, Shawn. Especially before the better teams on your schedule show up. You have to figure, Shawn, that everyone knows you are the key to the offense's success, and they also know you have a reconstructed ACL with a brace on it. Do you think they are going to stand back and let you pick them apart like 7-on-7 [drills]? No way, Shawn. Especially the 4A [largest] schools. They are going to say, 'Let's see if this boy can run, let's see how he does when we hit him in the mouth, let's try and knock him out of the game!' And that's football. Tune in for week one of the NFL season, Shawn, and count how many blitzes RG3 [Robert Griffin III, Washington Redskins quarterback, who also tore up a knee] faces until he proves he is the RG3 of old and you can't blitz him or he will burn you with his legs and arm."

* * * * *

Cary High School, a large-school 4A program, was the next opponent. My mom, younger sister Lauran, and brother Bruce came in for this game, to be played at Cary. Kate even loaded up Leo, Ella, and Jordan and came to the game. Our family has always shown up in droves when one of us plays in a sporting event; it is something I am most proud of about being a Stankavage. Cary ran a double wing offense, which is designed to use misdirection and deception in the running game to confuse the defense and control the ball for long periods of the game. Do it right, and the other offense won't see the ball nearly as much as it wants.

Gibbons struck first on a beautiful fake run and then a deep pass from Shawn to one of his wideouts, who had slipped uncovered behind the defense. It was 7-0 after the first drive; great start against a strong team. But then Cary quickly drove 70 yards—all runs, not a single pass—for a tying TD. It was an indication of things to come; Cary would be able to simply run at will and control the game.

On the next drive, Shawn underthrew a deep pass and it was intercepted. Cary couldn't be stopped on offense once again. It was 14-7. A Gibbons running back fumbled the next time CGHS had the ball, Cary drove to score again, and it was 21-7. In the end, the game got away from Gibbons, and Cary won 49-21. Shawn was 14 of 25 for 163 yards, but he had two interceptions again. He threw for two scores and ran for one. Not very impressive by the standards Shawn held for himself.

* * * * *

This was Shawn's first loss as a high school quarterback, and he took it hard. He did not play well, and the interceptions bothered him. Both were his fault for not making the proper throws. A quarterback has so many responsibilities and so many different ways to be evaluated. One metric is his decision-making and whether he was throwing to the right guy. Another is his execution and whether he made the proper and correct throw on time. Shawn's problem wasn't decision-making; it was his execution. On the interceptions he had not thrown the ball far enough and out of harm's way (throwing away from leverage). Shawn told Coach Wilson he was concerned with his play.

But the hardest part for Shawn was what happened in the team meeting to review game film the next morning. Shawn felt his coaches practically blamed the loss on him. He was distraught when he arrived home.

In the next class, Coach Wilson started the session by saying, "Shawn, the good news is you are 1-1 and not 0-2. . . . To me, it's obvious that for your team to win, the quarterback has to play, not only very well, but great, almost flawless. OK. That's where we are.

"Shawn, so you felt criticized after the loss? That happens. Here's the truth: the quarterback gets too much credit and he gets too much blame. It's a *team* game. There was plenty of blame to go around from what I saw on film. But can you play better? Yes, absolutely. Will you have to? Yes. But Shawn, you need to develop thicker skin. Remember, the toughest skins come from the toughest animals. You have to take the criticism and coaching and allow it to make you better and fuel your fire. Coaches always want to know how a player responds to adversity. This is your time to show the coaches and the team how you will respond.

"You have a tough assignment in the current environment you find yourself in. The good news is the Southern Durham game for first place isn't until October 11 [week 9 on the calendar], so in the weeks ahead you can get this all fixed. And what's more important is that you have done the work prior to the season and you are ready to step up and get things corrected. If you hadn't put in the work, it would be a different story—but you have.

"Remember, you can hardly ever control your environment, and when it's not what you wanted, you can't let it limit your future.

"One of the first lessons of being a great quarterback is to man up. Don't be always looking for sugar from the coaches or the media or the fans, especially when you lose or things don't go well. You learn to say 'yes sir' and 'no sir' to your coaches and just do better next time. You are a good quarterback, but you are working on being a great quarterback.

"So what are you going to do? Watch more film. Take more notes. Ask more questions. Read more defenses. Study your old notes. Superimpose your plays in your mind whenever you watch opposing defenses. Put your mind through the exercise of reading a defense pre-snap and then post-snap with every play you watch on TV.

"And you are prepared for this, Shawn. I am 100 percent confident in your preparation for your future."

Coach finished by pointing out that Shawn's mechanics of throwing and his kinesthetic awareness was not back to normal, so what he might think was the perfect throw would end up short because he was recalibrating his body to the new normal after the surgery and all the rehab. This was to be expected, Coach said. "Don't panic over this!" An important message, delivered with Coach's usual intensity, but also with grace.

* * * * *

The next two weeks were wins, the first against an outmatched Ravenscroft team, the second a thriller. Gibbons led city rival Broughton 27-0 at halftime, and that's usually a lock at most levels of football. But after failure at running the ball through much of the second half, four Crusaders fumbles, and a furious Broughton comeback, Gibbons trailed 28-27 with two minutes left. It was then that I saw an animated exchange between Shawn and his head coach on the sidelines. At one point, Shawn pounded his chest and turned from the coach. The head coach told a newspaper afterward that Shawn's words were, "I got this, Coach. Just let me have the ball."

And that is what Gibbons did, and Shawn did exactly what he told his head coach he would. He led an 80-yard drive in which he completed two third-down passes and then hit his wide receiver on a perfect deep post for a touchdown to win the game. Shawn finished 22 of 36 for 434 yards and three touchdowns while rushing 15 times for 91 yards. That is a 525-yard total offensive output. Shawn had been brilliant, and we were all proud.

After a bye week, Gibbons won its next three by margins of 28,

25, and 30 points. At 6-1, the team seemed fully recovered from the Cary loss.

* * * * *

On October 3, Shawn's 18th birthday, he was sitting at our kitchen table doing homework when his cell phone buzzed. "Hey Dad," Shawn said, turning and looking at me. "It says 'Wyoming football.'" I just looked at him like: *Well, you better answer it!* It was the University of Wyoming quarterbacks coach, Jason Gesser, who first made some small talk and then came out with a pronouncement that the Cowboys were going to offer Shawn a scholarship to play college football for them. Shawn's grin when he heard this news was something I will never forget. He gave a thumbs-up to me while he was still on the phone, and then he told the coach that he was extremely grateful and couldn't wait to learn more about the school and schedule a visit with his parents. All in all, not a bad way to celebrate your 18th birthday.

I think we all slept especially well that night. Shawn's first Division I offer was coming in, and that from a school with a coaching staff that knew how to throw the ball and evaluate quarterbacks. It was affirmation that all of Shawn's work was going to pay off.

The next game brought another easy win against an outmatched Oxford Webb High, and Gibbons was now 7-1.

* * * * *

Then came a powerhouse, Southern Durham, which was normally 4A in size but had slipped a bit in enrollment and was now 3A and in the same conference with Gibbons. Gibbons had won 22 straight conference games and had the home field advantage for this first-ever matchup between two stout programs. But Southern had five Division I recruits and was filled with fantastic, quick athletes; frankly, it was an intimidating team. Shawn had played with many of the SD players, or for their coaches, during his early years in Pop Warner football. One of Shawn's leadership roles that week was to help his team overcome any fear or anxiety. This game had a great competitive atmosphere.

Southern rolled out to a 31-7 lead, and still led 31-14 when Shawn led a scoring drive that ended just five seconds before halftime. Gibbons clawed back to 38-28 in the second half, but a late fumble ended any last hope for the home team. Shawn had another 400-plus-yard offensive night against what many thought was one of the top three teams in the state. A tough loss, but CGHS played and fought hard, and the team was still 7-2 overall.

And there was also the possibility of getting SD in a rematch in the state playoffs on the road to a state championship.

* * * * *

Chapel Hill was next, and this was a classic rebound game. It also could be called a "trap game," a matchup in which one team should win, but external reasons can easily lead to that team's downfall. Everything led in that direction for Gibbons. It was on cable TV and would be broadcast widely across the state as well, so Shawn and Gibbons wanted to look sharp, but they also were coming off the tough SD loss. And as one might have predicted, at halftime Gibbons trailed, and the score was 26-18.

The Crusaders were still down, 36-26, in the fourth quarter when they lined up in punt formation on fourth down, with Shawn back deep at punter. The game turned here, and again Shawn was able to show some magic. He rolled right on a fake punt, but was trapped and had no one to throw to ahead of him. Of course, being fourth down, he couldn't just throw the ball out of bounds. So Shawn reversed his tracks and ran all the way across the field and back to his left while continuing to look for an open receiver in the CGHS all-black. But there was no receiver to be found, so Shawn had to make a split-second decision: he turned upfield and juked the first defender, then saw an alley back to his right and burst through it like some kind of cat chasing his prey. Fifty-one yards later, he was knocked out of bounds at the 12-yard line. He then threw a touchdown pass to keep CGHS alive; this drive completely changed the momentum.

The Gibbons defense held, and on the last drive of the game, Shawn kept the ball on an option play and scored on a 9-yard TD run for the win, 39-36. Shawn threw for 214 yards and ran for 198 yards on 18 carries. Another 400-plus-yard game of total offense.

Coach Wilson called Shawn Superman during our class session in which we reviewed the game film; Shawn seemed to like the moniker. But Coach also had some highly technical and critical analysis of a few of Shawn's plays. He was particularly hard on him in evaluating three of Shawn's touchdown passes. On all three plays Coach stopped the video at the precise moment when it was clear the ball should have been thrown; each time Shawn was not ready to throw. His feet were not set, his base was too narrow, and the ball was not loaded in proper position for release. Consequently, it was thrown two or three steps later than it should have been.

The results were touchdowns, but on film Coach was making the point that it wasn't good enough. "If you hold the ball like this against Georgia or Alabama, all of these passes will be intercepted," Coach said.

Shawn got the message: this was about not only high school, but also preparing for the next level. There was always a method to Coach's teaching. As always, I was learning as much as Shawn.

TWELVE

Senior Season's Second Half

"The best is yet to come. I promise you that"

Late Fall

I pulled into the driveway at Shawn's mom's house at 4 a.m. on Saturday morning. I had tried to lay low all week to preserve my energy for this trip to see the University of Wyoming. I had gotten to bed after 11 p.m. following Shawn's Friday night game. So that means Shawn didn't get to sleep until closer to 1 a.m.

Shawn practically crawled into my car, throwing his pack in. It was early all right, and Shawn was going on maybe three hours of sleep. Not only was he beat from the previous night's game, but he also had to be beat from the weight of the entire season. I think he grunted, "What's up?" It was too early to talk about the game the night before.

Coach Wilson had schooled me pretty hard on the dos and don'ts of this trip. Coach knew that Shawn wasn't an early morning person. "So lay off him, Dad, until he wakes up," he said. This would be sometime after our layover in Charlotte as we headed to Denver. Once in Denver, we picked up a rental car. It was there that Shawn began to open up and loosen up. He had never seen the Rocky Mountains before, and they are majestic. The snow-caps were magnificent and the sky a clear, electric blue. I could see Shawn's enchantment with the big country, and I reminisced about my first time to Denver as a free agent quarterback, flying in right after my college graduation ceremony. I had the same awe in my eyes on my first trip to Colorado.

We drove through Fort Collins on our way to Laramie, Wyoming, and the flatness of the plains as they butted up against the Rockies became evident. We still had a long way to go, but we were enjoying the drive together.

As we approached Laramie we began to get excited for a college football game. The weather was cold, but not unbearable, and the sunshine bright. We drove into town through the main drag and realized we were on campus. We saw some academic buildings and then could see the traffic for the game up ahead, the stadium on the left. We picked a side street and parked in the first spot we could find, then hoofed it to the stadium.

The game was a blowout—and not in Wyoming's favor—so we left early and went to explore. First we headed to campus and tried to get a feel for the school. We had grabbed a bite to eat when my phone rang. It was Coach Gesser looking to meet with us after the game.

Jason Gesser came across as a quality coach, one whom I would consider entrusting with our son's future. He spent the next 90 minutes with us, showing us the sports facilities and introducing us to players and coaches that we ran into. The coaches were inviting, and all of them seemed to recognize Shawn and had great things to say about his highlight video. The players had similar things to say, told Shawn he would fit right in, and even added that they could use him next year. All of that made Shawn, and me, feel great.

By the time the visit was over, Shawn had a whole new perspective on, and interest in, the University of Wyoming. It was his only Division I scholarship offer at that point, but it was affirming because it had been offered by a school and a coach who had played the position at a high level (Gesser was a Rose Bowl quarterback at Washington State). It was exactly what I had hoped to accomplish with this visit.

That night we headed to Denver to find a hotel. We were excited to check out the University of Colorado the next day. I woke before Shawn the next morning and headed to the lobby to find a cup of coffee. My phone rang and it had a Kentucky area code. I let the call go to voice mail. It was Bobby Petrino asking me to call him about recruiting Shawn. I let Shawn continue to sleep and called back the Western Kentucky University head coach. (Petrino would move to the University of Louisville the following year.) Shawn would enjoy the news that another coach with a history of success with quarterbacks was interested in him.

After walking around the University of Colorado campus, we set out for downtown Denver. We circled the Denver Broncos' stadium and the memories came flooding back. We were even able to walk onto the field when a wonderful security attendant gave us permission after I told her of my history with the team. She even took our photo. It was a great memory for us and an exciting time for Shawn.

The night before, as Shawn drifted off to sleep, tears rolled down my cheeks as I reflected on the significance of this trip with my son. The leukemia, my career and my past, my son, his career and his future—all seemed to be right in that moment. I told Shawn how special it was for me to have made that trip with him, to come back to Denver, where my dreams had come true, and to share this experience with him. I could feel our connection, including his appreciation for me and my career and also his recognition of my huge and unending love for and pride in him.

I couldn't help but think of my father in that moment as well. We didn't have the relationship that I have with Shawn. I am a talker. My father was not. He never really gave me advice, but he was always there, at all my games, taking off work, passing up promotions, just so he could be at all four of his children's athletic events. That made an impact on me; it's something that resonates even more for me now that I'm a father of seven. I make a point to not only be a physical presence in my children's lives but to also speak into their lives as they grow.

We got back very late on Sunday from the whirlwind Wyoming trip—everything was accomplished in less than 48 hours. I let Shawn sleep in and go into school late on Monday morning.

* * * * *

The next challenge was Orange High School. Orange was undefeated, had the number one-ranked defense in the state, and played an extremely physical, hard-nosed game. Players had been ejected in last year's game for late hits against Shawn. This game would be for second place behind Southern Durham in the league standings, and Orange would play Southern in the last game of the year for first place if it won this game. Orange was a hungry team.

I was having a hard week. My chemo was in full session, and things were rough. I was putting up a good front for friends and family, but inside I was feeling slightly overwhelmed at the enormity of the prognosis and the possibility that I wouldn't be around long. I was also following the public stories of others who were battling cancer, including Indianapolis Colts head coach Chuck Pagano; fellow Tar Heel, women's basketball coach Sylvia Hatchell; and ESPN personality Stuart Scott. (Scott passed away from his cancer in January 2015.) But I often drew on this: I had been mesmerized by the famous Jimmy Valvano speech at the ESPY Awards, in which he laughed at the cameraman showing him a red light as he was on stage, as if his time was up. He then went on to say some of the most memorable words spoken in sports: Coach V, essentially dying of cancer, looked into the camera that night and said, "If you laugh, think, and cry every day, then it is a full day." And then he delivered his famous line of "Don't give up, don't ever give up." I remember watching that speech live and standing by myself in my living room to applaud Coach V for those amazing words.

Laugh, think, and cry. But I also knew cancer was a bitch to fight. Now I was in the middle of my own private session, and while I kept a good face for others, I was getting worn down inside.

* * * * *

Friday night, early November. The weather was cold and rainy and my doctors advised against going to the game. But it was archrival Orange, the playoffs were at stake, and the suggestion that I not go was the last thing I wanted to hear. "Over my dead body" was my response—but then, as I spent more time thinking about it, I realized I didn't need to be careless with my health in this battle. When I was first diagnosed, I asked one of the doctors at Duke, "How does leukemia actually kill you?" And he said, "Leukemia doesn't kill you, it depletes your immune system to the point that some other disease gets you because your body can't fight it." This weather, and my physical status after three months of chemotherapy, was the perfect storm for some type of infection to get into my system. I made the decision that I couldn't chance it. So I didn't go to the game—the only one I would miss in Shawn's entire football career.

That was a hard four hours, from the 7 p.m. kickoff until 11 p.m. when somebody could give me a report.

* * * * *

I remember the time exactly. My cell rang at 11:03 p.m. It was Shawn.

"Dad. I did all I could, gave it everything I had, but we still lost. I left it all on the field. You would have been proud."

My heart dropped to hear that the team lost, but there was a joy, a pride, and something was different in Shawn's voice than I had ever heard before. I think he knew that the score ultimately didn't define him as a player or as a young man. He knows how high my standards are, especially for him. So for him to speak with such confidence, I knew he had played a special game.

After being tied 28-28 at halftime, Orange eventually won 44-31, but not before Shawn nearly posted another 500-yard total offense game against this top-rated defense. He passed for 430 yards on 31 of 44, with two touchdowns, and ran for another 61 yards and one score. At one point he completed nine straight passes. In the paper the next day the Orange coach said, "Stankavage was too much for us in the first half; he came out and shocked us. He is one of the best quarterbacks, not only in North Carolina, but in the country. He is something special, and when he graduates, I am going to be there to make sure he walks across the stage so we don't have to play him again."

The next day Shawn and I watched some of the game film together. Number 10 in the white jersey was impressive, even by my critical standards. The local newspaper had a photo of Shawn being chased by an Orange defender under the headline, "Game of the Year."

I was so proud of Shawn. I was sad I had missed the game in person, but happy that he enjoyed the competition even in the loss. I think there was something unspoken between us regarding him playing and me not being there. Somehow he was showing off, making me proud, inspiring me in my fight, or something to that effect. I could sense it in his voice and in his words when he spoke to me that night after the game; it was another moment I will never forget.

For that Sunday night class with Coach, we went over the Orange game film. Coach didn't talk about anything technical in this session, he really just complimented Shawn on his courage and his relentless effort to make plays for his team, no matter the situation. He marveled at his ability to escape and his pocket presence and throwing mechanics even in the face of a strong pass rush. Shawn seemed proud to have earned such praise from Coach. It was the first and only game that neither I nor Coach would attend, and somehow that presented a different dynamic to Shawn. There was an element of *I can do this, even without my support team being physically there*. It was another big step in Shawn's growth.

After Shawn went upstairs following class, Coach was packing up when he said to me, "That was one of the best high school quarterback performances I have ever seen on film. That was no joke of a defense and he damn near beat them carrying as much of it as he could all by himself."

* * * * *

The final regular-season game was Northwood, and that meant senior night. The tradition is that after practice on Thursday night, all the fathers of the senior football players gather in the chapel just off the high school auditorium. On this night, there were twenty-two fathers gathered, each with notecards or folded papers with notes in their pockets. The ceremony itself is a wonderful idea by the head coach, one designed to publically affirm each boy in the voice of his father. Men cry. Sons cry. There is laughter and cheers.

When it was my turn, I stood at the front of the room, directly in front of Shawn. I looked at him and beamed with pride. My goal was to make my remarks short, concise, impactful, and memorable. Here were my exact words:

Shawn. It is a great honor that God asked me to be your father eighteen years ago. They say the measure of a man is not always what he accomplishes, but sometimes it is what he overcomes. By both standards, you have defined yourself a champion. From divorce, injury, parenting conflicts, and an ACL reconstruction less than a year ago, many wondered how you would respond this season. There are no questions now, as you have prevailed with an uncommon strength for someone your age. I couldn't be prouder. You inspire me, Shawn. . . . I don't know how many more games God has for me to see you play, but you are a five-star son and the top son in the country to me. Thank you for sharing my passion for football all these years, which has given me some of my greatest joys in watching and coaching you. You have represented yourself, our family, the Lord, and your teams with honor, integrity, and joy. I love you and am proud to be your father."

Northwood was a football program on the rise. It had a very good offense and a quarterback who put up big numbers. In the newspaper someone was quoted as saying that Stankavage was, essentially, overrated. Shawn had matured to the point that he just answered with his play. He threw for seven touchdowns, ran for another, and was 29 for 36 for 451 yards and another 65 yards of rushing; he didn't even play the fourth quarter. This was his fifth game with more than 400 yards of total offense and his third with more than 500. He was ranked 18th in the country in total offense per game.

Gibbons had finished a 9-3 regular season. The first round of the state playoffs was next.

* * * * *

Playoffs are always a gut-wrenching time, but there just isn't that much to say about this game. Gibbons was all business and won the game easily. The biggest story line of this playoff win, over Triton High School, was Shawn's request to switch jersey numbers from his usual 10 to the number 7 to honor a teammate who had missed the season with a knee injury; Shawn knew all about missing the heat of a playoff game because of an injury. It was an impressive gesture by an 18-year-old, and one that made me proud. I didn't know about it until game time. I joked afterward that he might want to think about keeping that 7 on his back. Shawn went 26 for 33 for 281 yards and five scoring throws while rushing 18 times for another 119 yards. Another game of 400 yards of total offense, and Gibbons was moving on.

* * * * *

It often seemed like there was a parallel between my battles and Shawn's.

My chemotherapy was scheduled so that I would receive IV treatments on Mondays and Wednesdays during the first week of the month, and then only on Monday the following week. Then I'd get a steroid cocktail the third week. The fourth week of the month was no treatment, except to monitor my blood count levels. So we did that pretty much through the entire high school football season.

Friends or family came to sit with me during the infusions, which always provided a boost. And fortunately, I was not being given cytotoxic chemotherapy, which is like napalming the entire immune system. One doctor said that if your blood is a garden and there are weeds in that garden, cytotoxic chemo is like using an industrial-strength spray to kill the entire garden and then hoping that the plants will grow back and not the weeds. But my protocol, and those of many cancer treatments today, was one of targeted chemistry, more like using a special herbicide designed to kill only the weeds in the garden and not the good fruit-bearing plants as well.

I was down to my last treatment and my body was responding well to the protocol that my doctors had prepared, so hope and thanksgiving were abundant. I told Kate that she did not need to go with me for the last treatments, and surprisingly, she did not resist. She had been by my side for every session, but I was able to convince her that it was OK if she didn't join me for a few treatments toward the end. It was good for Kate to have a break, and I enjoyed the time to reflect.

I checked in to the clinic for my last session and sat at the end of the waiting area where I could see the magnificent Duke Chapel that overlooks the entire campus and hospital. I always offered some prayers from that view. The Chapel also held special significance for me because it was on those outside steps that I asked Kate to marry me on Thanksgiving night 2004, and our three youngest children were all baptized in that sanctuary as well.

As I was praying, out of the corner of my vision I saw two people moving past the reception desk and walking toward me. I glanced their way out of habit, and then turned back toward the Chapel. But in that moment, I reshuffled my gaze and did a double take back toward the two.

It was Shawn and his sister Shelby. It was only fitting that they had come to surprise me for my last treatments, as Sarah and Bruce surprised me for my first. My eyes filled with tears of joy as I wrapped my arms around Shawn and Shelby and drew them close.

* * * * *

Shawn and his teammates got what they had wished for, another shot at Southern Durham in the state playoffs. This time, however, the setting would be even tougher as the game would be played at Southern Durham High School.

Shawn's text from the team bus heading into the stadium said: *Dad, it reminds me of my childhood with you when you would bring me up here on the sidelines with you when you coached here. This is where it all began.*

I texted back: *Don't let it end here, go and be Superman.*

And he did. It was an epic high school game, one for the ages, a game that anyone who saw it will never forget. It's a gift for an athlete to play in that kind of memorable contest. For Gibbons and SD, the athletes got such a gift on that November night.

It was such a big event that even Coach Wilson's 80-year-old mother dressed in warm clothes and came to the game, sitting with us at the top of the stands. When I asked her what she was doing out on a cold Friday night, she smiled and said, "I had to make sure I saw with my own eyes this quarterback my son has been talking about so much."

Things started well for CGHS; Southern couldn't have played worse in the first three quarters. Gibbons ran its standard spread offense with no huddle, but the Crusaders slowed the game down so that every snap would be taken with less than five seconds showing on the play clock. And this strategy worked; it kept the high-powered Southern offense off the field for long stretches, essentially shortening the game and giving Southern fewer possessions than it was used to. As each quarter went by, Gibbons' confidence grew.

But Gibbons had an undoing as well. It would have four red-zone possessions that came up without any points. Two or more such possessions almost always haunt a team; four is just too many.

With just 6:29 left in the game, Shawn finished a 70-yard touchdown drive that culminated in a fourth-down play that will live forever on YouTube. Shawn took the snap and tried to roll to his left, but a blitzing linebacker came through unblocked to take down Shawn. He tried to reverse his field and go back to his right to avoid being dropped, but slipped, and in the process Shawn was hit and fumbled the ball. A Southern player tried to scoop it up, but missed, and other Southern players began celebrating what they thought was a sack on fourth down. The ball was still squibbing around; it was a live ball. Shawn got up off the turf and had the sense, time, and savvy to pick up the ball and dash once again toward the goal line. After just two steps, he saw Dante DiMaggio in the back of the end zone with no defenders around. Shawn lifted an easy toss for the touchdown. The crowd went wild on the Gibbons side and dead silent on the Southern side. What just happened?! and *Did that really happen!?* were the sentiments of most people watching. I was next to Coach Wilson, and he just blurted out, with this look of total disbelief: "No he didn't . . . NO. HE. DIDN'T!!" I could only smile and think, *Yes, he just did.*

Gibbons now led 28-26. It kicked off, Southern muffed the kick, and the ball was on the 15-yard line. If Gibbons could stop SD one more time, the Crusaders would win and advance. But Kendall Hinton (a Wake Forest quarterback recruit and former Pop Warner teammate of Shawn's) showed why he was such a heralded player. He took SD 85 yards for the go-ahead score with just 42 seconds left. Gibbons' huge celebration balloon seemed to have loudly popped. We were all crestfallen, and I slumped in my seat, but I was also so proud of Shawn and all the boys to have come this close—it appeared to be a 33-28 last-minute loss for Gibbons.

Then it felt like we were in a movie, and someone stated that there was still a *chance.* That someone was Coach Wilson, who bumped me with his elbow. The moment is still kind of frozen in my mind. "Hold on there, brother. I see Superman in the house. What's he going to do? He's going to win this thing. Mark my words." Coach was smiling—calm and actually smiling.

I just blurted something like, "C'mon, Coach, he's got no

timeouts and 75 yards to go against bigger, faster, stronger guys."
Coach answered: "Hey man, Superman don't show up until the
situation is bleak and nobody else can get the job done. It's time,
and Shawn is in the house. Let's watch him work."

Coach had told Shawn a few times in our basement that legendary Dallas Cowboys coach Tom Landry would say, "Greatness is
the ability to make the play when you absolutely have to have it."
And that is what would be required in this moment.

After the kickoff, it was first and ten at the Gibbons 25. Shawn
brought his team to the line of scrimmage. . . . Completion and
out of bounds . . . then, completion and first down, and, as in
both high school and college rules, this stops the clock to move
the sideline chains. The ball was right at the 50, and 31 seconds
were left.

Next: incompletion . . . then, defensive blitz, and Shawn had to
scramble. He rolled left, stopped and reversed his field, and then
threw the ball out of bounds. Third and 10, still 50 yards away,
and just 19 seconds left. Once again, it was looking very bleak.

But then came a long completion in the middle of the field,
with the Gibbons receiver running toward the sidelines. He had
a first down and then broke a tackle! He had a shot at daylight
toward the end zone as the clock ticked . . . :00:05 . . . :00:04 . . .
:00:03 . . .

"Get out of bounds! Get out of bounds!" everyone seemed to
be yelling.

The Gibbons receiver tried to cut back to get to the end zone,
but was tackled in the field of play. . . . The referee blew his whistle to stop the clock and move the chains. The game clock showed
1.8 seconds left. The ball was on the 12, and both teams rushed
to the line of scrimmage. The rules state that when both teams
are set, the referee will blow his whistle and the clock will start.
Unless Gibbons was ready, the game could be over without a center snap back to Shawn.

But Shawn knew this, ran forward to his center, and shouted
in his ear, "No matter what, when the referee blows his whistle to
put the ball in play, you just snap it to me—immediately."

And he did. Gibbons had somehow gotten lined up in its standard double-slot formation. When the whistle blew, the center snapped the ball to Shawn. . . . It was all now a blur . . . and then another whistle blew and everyone on the field stopped . . . . Shawn looked toward the referee, who was behind him in the backfield, and the man in the black-and-white shirt shrugged his shoulders . . . and motioned for Shawn to play on.

This wasn't going to be a sane ending; chaos was breaking loose. At that same moment, the Southern sideline heard the whistle and thought the game was over. Its players came running onto the field to celebrate a victory. And nine of eleven players on defense had stopped playing. But when Shawn saw the back judge motion for him to keep playing, he rolled to his right and motioned to his wide receiver to go into the end zone. A defensive lineman started to chase Shawn, so he continued rolling to his right and threw the ball toward Dante DiMaggio. Again, it was like something in a movie, and time seemed to slow. . . . As the ball approached, the only other Southern defender who was alert enough to keep playing was covering Dante and, at the last moment . . . reached out and tipped the ball . . . causing it to bounce off the receiver's hands and shoulder pads . . . and fall to the ground. Incomplete.

It was surreal. Everyone was in shock, stunned. Did the play actually count? Was the game over? What would the referees do? The field was flooded with not only the twenty-two players who were in the game, but also with half the Southern Durham team from off the sidelines as well. The Gibbons coaches ran toward the refs, who were huddling at the hash marks at about the 10-yard line to figure out what had happened and what to do.

They were obviously trying to weigh the fact that one of them had blown the play dead after the whistle to start the clock, and that almost all the Southern defenders had stopped. One of the referees was pushing players and coaches back from the referee huddle, trying to give the officials privacy and the ability to communicate and sort things out. And now it was a waiting game . . .

After a minute, and in the midst of a huge crowd of mostly

Southern Durham fans, the group of referees broke from their huddle and the head referee took the ball and waved it in the air in a circular motion, the signal for the end of the game. My heart sank as I watched the six men in striped shirts hightail it off that field faster than they had run all game, their decision final. It was truly bizarre.

Southern players and fans celebrated in delirium.

Gibbons players and fans cried on the field and in the stands.

Shawn's high school career was over. It ended on the same field where his football dreams were born.

I walked around the fence to the track and went onto the field to find Shawn and give him a hug. I found him on one knee at the 40, head down and crying. I knelt and put my arm around him and said, "I love you, dude. I could not be more proud of you, not only for tonight, but your entire high school career. You are a warrior and a champion."

Shawn said, "I love you too, Dad. I can't believe it's over. It's all over."

I just squeezed his neck, holding back my own tears, and said, "Son, the best is yet to come. I promise you that. The best is yet to come."

* * * * *

Southern would go on to win the state championship three weeks later. And many of their players and coaches would say that Gibbons was their toughest opponent all year and that Shawn was the best player they faced in their championship season.

THIRTEEN

Suddenly a Hot Commodity

"Betting on yourself . . . "

December–February, Shawn's Senior Year

Late fall led to a decision from Shawn to skip his senior season of basketball. I didn't originally agree with this call, but there were several reasons Shawn felt he had to make it, which I won't list here. For a brief time I lobbied that he play, in part to display his athleticism to football coaches, as I know this had helped my recruitment out of high school. I even shared a quote from Ohio State University head football coach Urban Meyer saying how he loves to recruit two-sport athletes, and the majority of his players are just that. But Coach Wilson was pleased with Shawn's decision and suggested it was the right one.

It all worked out for the best as Shawn ended up being able to participate in a number of additional quarterback classes with Coach during December; these covered numerous topics about college football that offered valuable insights and preparation for the upcoming recruiting season. Or so we hoped.

Opportunity

It was just before Christmas and the three of us were in class in the basement once again. Coach's theme this evening was opportunity. "Opportunity rarely comes when we expect it," Coach said. And he took off from there.

"So, what is going on? Colleges see your six-foot-two, 185-pound body on film and don't think it is Division I-ready, Shawn. And it isn't today. And they wonder, 'Why hasn't he done the work in the weight room to get ready? So, will he?'

"Shawn, you have to realize that opportunity rarely comes in the ways you expect. So the key is to be prepared when the opportunity comes. And preparation takes place in the dark, away from the spotlight. It is now a matter of what you do when no one is looking. How driven will you be? It's up to you. You have the talent, I am sure of that. Now you must find the drive.

"Opportunity is also not usually what it appears at first glance. A man must evaluate opportunity based on what it could become and where it can take you. Many people come to a fork in the road of opportunity and don't take it because they don't have the vision to see where it could lead them—they only see that it wasn't what they expected or wanted. And here again, preparation is the key.

"Did you do the work before you were tested? It's one thing to get the test and then realize what you need to do. But it's another thing altogether to get the test and have already done the preparation. That's when you ace the test and go to the next level. In life, always do your homework before it is required!"

* * * * *

In another class in early January, Coach educated Shawn on all things recruiting: projecting himself and his voice in interviews and in discussions with college coaches . . . expressing himself clearly . . . just pure confidence. I shared with Shawn and Coach a quote I found in which a Big Ten head coach talked about Wisconsin quarterback Russell Wilson, now a superstar and Super Bowl-winning quarterback with the Seattle Seahawks.

He said that Wilson had *swag*. "Man, he had it in warm-ups," this coach said. "Not cocky. Just confidence. He had it. And he carried himself in a way that he knew that you knew that he had whatever it took to beat you on that day."

That's not for every young man to project in every interview, but there are things to imitate there, for sure. "Coaches are not fully objective," Coach told Shawn. "They have favorites. You gotta change somebody's mind about you!"

And Coach quickly moved back to what Shawn would need, mentally, to make the leap to the next level.

"You have been labeled consistently as a development guy with great, clean mechanics and playmaking mobility, but consensus is that your body isn't ready. But let me assure you, what you have, your talent and skills, can get them what they want. They just can't see that now. So maybe the time isn't right for you. But it *is* the time for your inner drive to kick into overdrive—with what you eat, what you lift, and how you get into your notes and train your mind on NFL-level football knowledge. Now is the time, Shawn! So that you are prepared to compete and win when you get your chance, wherever that may end up being."

Coach took a quick trip back to when he was a youngster just gaining a name for himself in high school.

"Everybody at my school knew I was committed to gaining weight. Classmates and even teachers all gave me their extra milk, every day. I would have fifteen or sixteen milks; I am not kidding you! I *destroyed* dozens of tennis balls in my pocket, squeezing them hourly in school to make my hands stronger. Remember: whatever it takes, and then a little bit more.

"So, what will be your secret? What is it that you will be willing to do when no one else is watching? What is it that you will do to help prepare you to win the job, to prevail against the competition when you need it most? If you don't do it now, it won't be there when that time comes to win the job, and that opportunity will be handed to someone who is better prepared."

Coach relayed a conversation he had had with one of his former players who was now a college coach. They had discussed

Shawn and his football career.

"One of my old players asked me yesterday, 'Coach, what if Shawn doesn't want it as bad as you do?' And here's what I told him: 'Doesn't matter to me. My calling and commitment is to give Shawn everything I have, to empty my toolbox for him to use if he wants to. My commitment is between me and God and all the people who have helped me in my life. I owe it to them. What Shawn does with it is between him and God as well . . . not between him and me. If anything, I am giving Shawn all I have to give out of respect for David Parker. He is the one who came and got me every day when I was ten years old and my parents had just gotten divorced and I was kinda lost. He drove all the way out to Northern Durham, where I lived, and took me to the John Avery Boys and Girls Club over on Alston Avenue so I could play sports. Eventually, they got a bus that took all of us from my neighborhood down to the Boys Club, but it was Mr. Parker that picked me up by himself those first few months. And so it is Mr. Parker that I am doing this for. I am just paying his belief in me forward.'"

Shawn was dialed in, listening intently at this point.

Coach had more on the focus Shawn needed—and even other options he might choose.

"Hey man, don't lose any sleep over your situation. If it comes down to it, you can go JUCO [junior college], or post-grad. Find the right spot and play another season and re-market yourself. Or, you can work out this summer and fall and enroll as a mid-year guy in January . . . and carefully take your time to select the program that best suits your skills and your needs and desires. This is a lifetime decision, Shawn. Don't be rushed into it. Your options are actually wide open.

"But, if you get to February 4 [national signing day, 2014] and don't like the options, then you have to say 'no thank you' and go back to work. And you know what that is called? *Betting on yourself.* Just like on Friday nights. Do you want the ball in your hands on offense to win the game, or would you rather score with one minute left and leave it up to your defense and the other quarterback? You know the answer: you want the ball! You bet on yourself!

"And I would too. But the thing that can block you is *doubt*. Doubt in yourself, doubt in your skills, doubt in what you know to be true. Doubt brings worry and affects effort and concentration and commitment. You must stay focused on gaining weight, studying your quarterback book, and getting better at presenting and projecting yourself. You have time. You are right on time, Shawn. But doubt is an enemy you want to identify and defeat. And it's not easy."

I couldn't help but resonate with everything Coach was telling Shawn. And for me, I could hear my favorite rock and roll singer, Bruce Springsteen, singing the last line to his song "Brilliant Disguise," which says, *God have mercy on a man who doubts what he is sure of.*

Coach continued: "The fact is that every major college program already has their quarterback recruit that they bought into last summer when you weren't even in the mix. Hey, you were overlooked, plain and simple. But you must not let that define you or be the final chapter."

Overlooked

Then Coach told a story that hit both Shawn and me hard.

"Shawn, let me tell you about being overlooked. When I was 10, I was an all-star in the Boys Club flag football league, but we didn't have an all-star game. I played in a league with all black kids. The other league, which was all white kids, picked an all-star team and they played a game to celebrate. Well, one of the guys on the chamber of commerce knew my mom and dad and suggested that they let me play in the other league's all-star game. So I went to practice, but they never taught me a single play. Truth is, I don't even think the coaches knew my name. I just stood there at practice for three straight days. I told my mom I wasn't going to play in the game, but she said I had committed to it, so she was going to make me go.

"On Saturday during the game, the same thing happened. For

over three quarters I stood by myself watching all the other boys play. Finally, in the fourth quarter, the referee came up to the head coach and said, 'Hey, remember, everybody has to play at least one play.' He was obviously referring to me, standing at the other end of the field. So the coach calls me over and says, 'Hey, we are going to put you in and toss you the ball to the right. You catch it and just run as best you can.'

"Reluctantly, I went into the game, and when they tossed me the ball, I went 75 yards for a touchdown. I tossed the ball back to the referee, but none of my teammates really celebrated with me. We were probably going to lose anyway because we were still down one touchdown and an extra point. So I went to the sidelines, and stood there again. The defense stopped the other team, so we got the ball back. The head coach called me over to go back in, but another coach came up and said, 'Hey, he had his play, he's done.' So I stood there. We ran three plays and gained no yards. So the head coach called me over on fourth down and said, 'Go back in and run the same toss play, OK?' So I did, but this time, when I caught the toss from the quarterback to the right, the entire defense was over there, so I reversed my field and ran for a 70-yard touchdown around the left side. Everybody cheered and jumped on me this time in the end zone, even though none of them knew my name.

"Now all we needed to win was the extra point. So the coach called the toss sweep to me one more time. I started right, was blocked off, reversed field back to the left, but there were two boys back there too, so I stuck my foot in the ground and cut right up the middle. I walked into the end zone to score the two-point conversion and we won the game. I was given the MVP certificate for that game, which I didn't even want to play in."

Shawn and I just sat there, not sure what to feel about the emotional impact of that story. Coach let the weight of the story hang there for a minute and then he spoke again.

"Do you know what the first page of my scrapbook is? Not the two Super Bowls, or the Hall of Fames I am in. Nope. The very first page, the most satisfying thing I have in that book, is that certificate: MVP of that all-star game when I was ten. So don't tell me about being overlooked. Because at the end of the day, it doesn't matter. I know what it's like to be overlooked. It makes you do extraordinary things, things you didn't know you could do. But you have to be ready when you get the chance. You have to be ready."

* * * * *

A couple of weeks later, Shawn came home to our house and told me that his high school coach said that coaches from the American and Colonial athletic conferences were going to call and talk about a scholarship offer. The phone never rang. Then Shawn's coach relayed that a few FCS (football championship subdivision) schools were going to visit and offer. Again, our phone never rang. I was bewildered. How could college coaches tell a high school coach one thing, not follow up, and allow such a bad impression to ensue? Recruiting was baffling and beyond frustrating to our family.

Something seemed funny, if not fishy, about the entire process. Shawn received virtually no recruiting mail. In my time, I remember nearly every day going into the guidance counselor's office or my head coach's office to see which schools had sent me a calendar or other promotional material about their school. I would take it to class and share it with all my buddies, who enjoyed the process along with me. But for Shawn, there was no mail, not at home, nor at the high school. The explanation was that colleges now reach out through social media and on the Internet, but to not have any mail—when we heard other prospects had baskets full of correspondence—left us befuddled.

Shawn ended the season among the top 20 quarterbacks nationally in total offense. He ended his senior season passing for more than 3,500 yards and 37 touchdowns and rushing for more than 1,300 yards and 14 scores. That's almost 5,000 yards of total offense and 51 touchdowns by one player. Wouldn't somebody want that kind of production in college at some level?

Coach Wilson kept telling Shawn to continue to work out

with intensity and to keep getting good grades, and he promised Shawn that something would break. After the college season, Coach said, various coaches would be fired, new ones hired, and there would be last-minute shakeups in the recruiting boards across the country. Coach insisted that Shawn would get his chance.

* * * * *

Just before national signing day, the North Carolina State quarterback coach stopped by Gibbons High School and met with Shawn. Was an offer forthcoming? Shawn relayed that the conversation went this way. The coach started with, "We hear that you would be interested as a walk-on at State. We would love to have you, and we think you can compete for our starting job."

Shawn said he asked the coach, "Is that what you came here to tell me, that you want me to walk on?" The coach reiterated the offer, but Shawn said he had other plans. End of that discussion. Shawn was furious.

But just as Coach had predicted, after the bowl games ended, numerous coaching shifts began to take place. Head coaches shifted at several major programs, including Texas, Louisville, Florida, USC, and Wake Forest. All of which, in a fortuitous game of musical chairs, led to East Carolina University needing a quarterback from Shawn's recruiting class. ECU had been one of Shawn's top three original picks and had stayed in soft contact with him throughout the season. ECU quickly rekindled a relationship with Shawn and began recruiting him hard those weeks before signing day. He took an official visit to Greenville with his mom, and said he could really see himself playing there. And before we knew it, Shawn had accepted a scholarship offer. It was exciting. It was the exact thing Shawn had been working toward.

* * * * *

Later in January, head coach Gary Kubiak was let go by the NFL Houston Texans, which then hired the Penn State coach, which led to the Vanderbilt coach going to Happy Valley. The result of all those coaching changes was that Vanderbilt, Shawn's number one school from day one, would have a new head coach. Things just got interesting. The Internet was on fire, and rumors were going strong that the Vanderbilt selection committee knew who it wanted for the school's next head coach: someone who could model the program after the success that Stanford was enjoying in the Pac 12.

Within a week, Vanderbilt hired Derek Mason, the former defensive coordinator at Stanford.

In the following week, Vanderbilt named a former NFL quarterback coach as offensive coordinator, and the next day Shawn got a call from the new Vanderbilt OC asking if he would be interested in coming to Nashville to play football in the SEC.

It appeared that Shawn was the recipient of some well-timed good fortune, and it felt like he was due for some! This is the kind of thing that, all along, Coach had said could happen if Shawn would keep working and believing. In a recent class, Coach had gone into preacher mode, telling Shawn and I, "The key is to do everything you can, and a little bit more, every day, because if you keep your head down long enough, one day you are going to pull right up alongside opportunity like pulling up your car at a traffic signal. And all you need to know is that you are ready and that you are prepared to take advantage of that moment. And if you are, then you jump in the car with opportunity and drive away. And if you aren't, the light turns green and opportunity drives away without you, and you may never pull up on it again. The key is to be prepared when it happens to you."

Shawn had accepted the earlier offer and made a verbal commitment—but verbal only—to play at ECU. But when Vanderbilt offered and that news got out into the recruiting world, suddenly Shawn was a hot commodity. Wake Forest sent its quarterback coach to school to watch Shawn throw. BYU called, and so did Tennessee. The Volunteers even sent their quarterback coach to Durham for an in-home visit. They wanted Shawn to come on a formal recruiting weekend to Knoxville. The problem was there was only one weekend left before the national signing day, and all official visits had to be completed by midnight the following Sunday. The coach suggested Shawn switch his planned visit to Nashville and Vanderbilt to come and see UT in Knoxville. Shawn was intrigued, and so was I. We left things that we would stay in contact with the UT coach while we were at Vanderbilt. We would see how things played out over that final official-visit weekend.

* * * * *

The crazy part is that when Shawn got the scholarship offer from Vanderbilt, and they asked him to come visit the campus the last weekend before signing day, he was so emotionally drained by the whole recruiting process that he told me he wanted to stick with his commitment to ECU. He was not interested in the Vanderbilt trip! I know my son, and I knew Vanderbilt had been his top school from the get-go. The truth was that Shawn felt pressure and loyalty to the ECU coaches. He hated the conflict that had quickly brewed, and he was glad to have accepted an offer and be done with any uncertainty. It had been a long, arduous journey on the recruiting front, and he was glad to bring it to closure. And ECU was a good choice.

Shawn and I had more than a few heart-to-heart conversations in the hours that led up to the final recruiting weekend. He eventually agreed to at least take the official Vanderbilt visit. I told him that I strongly believed that not going would be a premature call for the wrong reasons. I suggested it would have been like 10-year-old Steve Wilson refusing to go into that all-star game to take the toss from the quarterback. He just couldn't do that.

What parents who are new to the recruiting process don't fully understand is that none of this is really about the hearts of their sons. College football is a two-billion-dollar industry, and it is big business. Recruiting is more about the college programs, the coaches and their jobs, and their success—or lack of—in winning football games on Saturdays in the fall. It's about a coach being recognized as a good recruiter, about his school winning the recruiting game in the early spring, and then about winning on those 12 football Saturdays each fall. It's a big machine designed around the money of TV contracts and the sport of college football making the revenue to support entire athletic programs on the collegiate level. It doesn't look like this from the outside, sitting in the stands or watching ESPN while cheering on your team. But behind the scenes, it's not a pretty business. Eighteen-year-olds and their parents are mostly wide-eyed and big-hearted dreamers coming out of high school, and unfortunately, they are often the fodder of an industrial machine called college recruiting.

It was my job to protect Shawn's heart in this process as best I could. Because the fact of the matter is that those players who are identified as top-rated have a tremendous burden to carry and manage, while those who are not selected are left to wonder what happened—and why not them. In a counter-intuitive way, I think the advantage might actually be with the under-recruited, because being in that spot stokes the fire in their bellies, and they don't have the distraction and responsibly of all the hype and the interviews and the constant recruiting. We could see now that Shawn's under-recruitment was actually a blessing for his development.

The unfortunate part of recruiting is that it has become a season and a game unto itself; there are "winners" and "losers" each February on signing day. The media and the fans keep score and track the rankings and stars of their recruits versus their rival schools and then throw parties about getting so-and-so versus so-and-so. It can be a game, one big commercial game. The reality is that recruiting is the part of the season when fans get to participate. And they do, on Facebook and Twitter and Instagram. Fans contact the top recruits and flood the blogs with opinions and observations that create an avalanche of hype.

But in the end, it is all distraction. It's hard to see that when, as a family, you are in it for the first and likely only time. It's easy to get carried away and lose perspective. In truth, there's no exact science to recruiting or evaluating young talent, especially at quarterback. If there were, we wouldn't see so many first-round busts at quarterback in the NFL draft. And in recruiting, it's impossible to measure what is in a young man's heart, and to project what he will be at 21 years of age when he is 16 or 17. That's why it's an art, not a science, and that's why the best teachers and motivators have a great advantage in getting the most out of their players, no matter their ranking or rating.

* * * * *

The Vanderbilt recruiting weekend was exciting for the whole family.

On Saturday, Shawn and I met the coaches for breakfast. Shawn's mom flew in at lunchtime and we all met with academic advisors and toured the campus; we were told clearly that academics leads the way at Vanderbilt. Shawn got to hang out with fifteen other recruits, and we could see a bond developing between the young men.

On Saturday night there was a huge dinner and the athletic director and chancellor spoke to the group. When Coach Mason spoke and they showed a football highlight video, I had tears in my eyes; I was ready to sign up myself. After dinner Shawn said to me, "How could I not go here?" I smiled, paused, and then said, playfully, "Because you didn't think you were good enough." He rolled his eyes at my remark, also in a playful manner. I took that as affirmation that he had made his decision. His mom and I were delighted.

But later in the night, in a text to his mom, Shawn indicated he wasn't certain. We had to let him make his own decision, but I couldn't imagine what was going on in his head.

Sunday morning, I was up early. I was actually speaking to a Super Bowl breakfast gathering at a Raleigh church that morning. I had committed to the event before Shawn was invited on this official visit; the organizers understood my priority to be with Shawn and accommodated me by allowing me to speak to the group via phone over loudspeakers. I think the talk went well, but it was one of the more difficult I have ever given, not being able to see any audience reaction. In a Q/A session, I was asked my prediction on the Broncos-Seahawks Super Bowl. Being a Bronco alumnus and Peyton Manning fan, I was all in on the Broncos. (We all know how that turned out, the Seahawks and Russell Wilson drubbing my Broncos 43-8.)

A little later that morning, the Vanderbilt coaching staff would hold a group breakfast in a ballroom. A schedule was posted as to who would meet with Coach Mason for a final talk to end the recruiting weekend. Shawn was scheduled for 10 a.m. As I sat there, I saw two of the recruits come in with their parents and spend fifteen minutes behind closed doors, and then come out with Mason. He would say, loudly, "Anchor Down!"—a signal that the young man was signing with Vanderbilt, and the room would explode in applause. This, in other words, was the close of the sale.

This was a moment of truth, and something Shawn, Coach, and I had worked so hard and long for. And now Shawn seemed to be vacillating.

I went up to my room and called Coach Wilson. I described the situation, and he listened intently. "I don't know what Shawn is going to tell Coach Mason when he asks him point blank if he is in or not," I said.

"That's a problem," Coach said. "It's is not the way to handle the situation. You need to get to Shawn and explain what is going on and the gravity of handling it correctly. If he doesn't want to go to Vanderbilt, that's fine. But don't walk into that room not knowing. Being indecisive is not a good impression for an SEC quarterback prospect."

I called Shawn and woke him up. The boys had stayed out late the night before. I asked him if he was aware his meeting with Coach Mason was at 10. He groggily answered yes and said he'd be there.

I asked Shawn if he knew the extreme importance of this meeting, and told him he needed to make a decision. There was silence. I then asked what he was going to say to Coach Mason, and he said, "I don't know."

My heart raced. *We have come all this way over the past 16 months, and you don't know? Lord help me,* I thought.

I asked Shawn to meet his mother and me immediately, as soon as he could get ready, in the lobby. He didn't want to at first, but agreed. While Sue and I waited, I brought her up to speed. I asked her what she thought. Sue said, "Well, he has to make up his own mind. It's his decision."

I said, "I agree, but it's not the time to wait or gather more information or play it cool. Too much is at stake in this moment." She said she believed that it was still ultimately Shawn's call on how to handle. "He is a grown-up and has to make his own choices," she said.

When Shawn stepped off the elevator, I asked if we could move to an empty room, pull up three chairs, and sit and discuss this together. I asked Shawn where he stood and he said, "I will tell Coach Mason I had a great time and really like everything and that I want to go home and think about it."

I said, "OK, what could stop you from saying yes?" Things were starting to get a little tense; this was the crucial moment. Shawn answered, "Didn't you always teach me to take time to make decisions? That I should go back and check with my parents and family before anything major?"

"Yes, I did," I answered. "But here we are, your mom and I, right here. Let's get it all out on the table." I paused for a moment. "If you don't think you can play in the SEC, I understand. These are grown-ass men and this is no-joke football. Is that a factor?"

"No, Dad. I can play here!" He looked at me with an incredulous scowl. "I want to come to Vanderbilt." He talked about sitting with some of the other recruits the night before and how they all made a commitment to each other to come to Nashville and win. "So, I am in," Shawn said.

I said, "Congratulations. Now you just have to tell Coach Mason. Well done. SEC football at the Harvard of the south." I was smiling ear to ear.

Shawn smiled and hugged me. I reached toward his mom and drew her into the three-way hug. I kissed both my son and his mom on the head. I said, "I am proud of us. What a great moment, Shawn. We love you very much."

A short time later, as we walked into that breakfast, several coaches made eye contact. The point was obvious: they were wondering if we were in.

In a few moments, Coach Mason motioned for Shawn from the corner room. I followed Shawn and his mom into the room; the quarterback coach was also there. We sat in front of a table that was set up like a desk, with Coach Mason seated behind. This is a rare moment, and not many high school athletes get to experience something like this.

Coach Mason started the exchange and told Shawn he had been watching him the entire weekend. He said, "I watched the way you walked and ate and interacted with coaches and the staff and parents and players and the other recruits. It all matters, Shawn, especially for a guy that we want to lead the entire program."

Isn't this exactly what Coach had told us, I thought. But I was also wondering where he was going with his remarks. Was Coach Mason impressed? Or was he going to drop a bomb and say, "I didn't see what I needed to."

Here was another moment of truth. Coach Mason went on: "And Shawn, I liked what I saw. You have what I call swag. It's confidence, but it's not cocky. And I like what I see on tape when you play. I see the freedom and creativity and the same confidence to try anything to make a play. And that is what we need: we need a leader with moxie, a leader that the team will follow into battle, because they know that he can get it done. We want you here, Shawn. So what do you say? Are you coming to be a Commodore?"

I thought I knew what the end was, but the suspense was just as thick as a movie plot playing out . . . until it actually happened.

And in this moment, Shawn was smiling. It felt like ten seconds went by, and I was screaming inside, *Tell him yes!*

"Yes sir, Coach. I am coming to Vanderbilt to win an SEC championship."

Coach Mason said, "All right. Anchor down."

I was so excited, and there were hugs around the room. The Spirit came over me and I asked if we could pray. Coach Mason graciously said, "Absolutely," so we all put our hands on one another's shoulders. I led what felt like a truly meaningful moment in prayer. It wasn't me. It was God. And it was unlike anything I had felt. Thankful for a dream come true, for Shawn, and for our whole family.

And within a minute Coach Mason was coming through those double doors into the banquet room and yelling, "Anchor down!" There was applause. It was a special moment.

* * * * *

We went to the bookstore and loaded up on Vanderbilt gear, buying shirts for Shawn's brother, sisters, and cousins. It's safe to say I spent a good bit of money that morning.

Ironically, after lunch, my phone rang and there was a message from the University of Tennessee quarterback coach asking me if we were interested in coming to Knoxville for a visit and scholarship offer. I was flattered for Shawn to finally be wanted by multiple schools. I relayed this call to Shawn and asked him his thoughts. He said, "Dad, I am a Commodore now."

I was proud of him for that answer and how he had handled the entire process. Dreams really do come true, even at the last minute, to those who keep the faith and do the work.

After an All-American career as a wide receiver at Howard University, Steve Wilson made the 1979 Dallas Cowboys roster as a rookie free agent wide receiver. He is shown here in 1980 after he converted to defensive back at the urging of head coach Tom Landry.

PHOTO BY STEVE HARRIS

45 • Steve Wilson
Cornerback
DALLAS COWBOYS

Steve Wilson was a member of the Denver Broncos as a defensive back from 1982-1989, playing in two Super Bowls under head coach Dan Reeves. He scores on a touchdown on a fake punt during the 1986 season.

Now Coach Wilson, Steve huddles on the sidelines with his offensive players during the 1996 Heritage Bowl in Atlanta, Georgia. Howard beat Southern, 27-24.

After a record-setting career as a quarterback for the University of North Carolina Tar Heels, Scott Stankavage was a member of the Denver Broncos as a backup quarterback behind Hall of Famer John Elway and Gary Kubiak from 1984-1986. He rolls right in a 1984 game against the Chicago Bears.

*As a junior, Shawn Stankavage led Cardinal Gibbons High
School to a 12-0 record before suffering a torn ACL in a
playoff game. After his return from injury, during his senior
season, he passed for 3,585 yards, completing 223 of 349 (64
percent) for 34 touchdowns. He also rushed for 1,102 yards
on 152 attempts (7.3 per carry) and 15 touchdowns. Shawn
ended his two-year high school career with more than 7,500
yards of total offense and 88 touchdowns.
The wristband on Shawn's left wrist says, "Stay strong,
Dad"—a reference to Scott's battle with leukemia.*

Coach Wilson, Shawn, and Dad on national signing day at Cardinal Gibbons High School after Shawn signed his letter of intent to attend Vanderbilt University on a football scholarship.

FOURTEEN

The Class: Graduation

"Dad, I am proud of you . . . He is ready"

July

We all returned home from Nashville riding about three feet off the ground. Later that week, on national signing day, Cardinal Gibbons High School held a press conference and recognized 14 student-athletes who would accept college scholarships. Each gave a speech, and then there was time for the media and interviews. Coach Wilson and I were there, along with several others who coached Shawn throughout his career, from Pop Warner to AAU basketball. It was a memorable day.

Shawn had a typical case of "senioritis" as he finished his academic year. His mom stayed on him to finish strong because Vanderbilt University is no joke academically, and she didn't want him to put his acceptance in jeopardy if his grades slipped at all that final semester.

Shawn took the requisite beach trips and lifted with his old high school teammates as well. And then he said his good-byes and left for summer school at Vanderbilt. His mom and he drove the eight hours through the Appalachian Mountains from

Durham to Nashville and got Shawn settled in. It was a good introduction to college life, having one class to take and living and working out with the football team. I am glad he had the chance to get oriented and make a transition to college life in that way.

When the first session of summer school was over, Shawn came home for the weekend.

* * * * *

It was the July 4th weekend, and Hurricane Arthur had just glazed over the east coast of North Carolina the day before Shawn flew back from Nashville. When I saw Shawn, I asked him about his feelings on being home, and he told me it was great to be back and to just relax and do nothing for a few hours.

I told him—almost as an act of foreshadowing, or previewing, for him—that there is an old saying that "you can never go back home." And that Shawn would begin to recognize the changes in himself and in home as he knew it growing up. This was just part of a new season of life he had entered, and this is quite normal, I told him. I think he understood. I didn't say anything more, leaving the topic for future visits between my son and me. The truth of the matter was that I was the one who was going to have the larger void to fill. There would be no more going to watch him practice, no more weekly class sessions with Coach Wilson to review game or practice film. No more washing his sweaty workout jerseys or putting glasses of protein shakes I had mixed in front of him every half-hour when he was at my house so he would gain weight. In some ways, I was probably talking to myself about the future as much as I was to my son. I think it's a hard transition for most every parent, when your high schoolers go off to college. Fortunately, we had Leo, Ella, and Jordan to keep us busy, because there is no void in our house when they are awake!

* * * * *

For scheduling reasons that involved our ability to get wide receivers and coordinate with two other quarterbacks, Coach

Wilson had set up a session on a local turf field for noon on the Saturday afternoon of that holiday weekend. It was 96 degrees when I got out of my car, grabbed my green mesh bag with footballs and cones, my cooler with water bottles for the boys, and headed to take a seat in the bleachers. As I sat down on the metal, my bottom burned, and I quickly stood up to place a towel to sit on. Wow, it was *hot*. I thought: *What if I was called to do this workout today?* I quickly concluded I wouldn't! I was too old and too fatigued from leukemia, and there was nothing in me that would have driven me to work out in this heat. I was just happy to be there to watch the session. And to be honest, it took all I had to attend.

And then I realized—not for the first time, but in a more meaningful and significant way—that a transition had been made. A shift had taken place between Shawn and myself. There had been days when it felt like I had to put in as much effort as Shawn to get him to keep working to take the next step, but we were so far past that now. From here on out, it was 100 percent about Shawn and his drive and his passion and his pursuit of his dreams.

Sitting there on the bleachers, I heard a beep-beep from a horn coming into the parking lot. It was Shawn's Explorer, windows down, country music thumping. He waved as he turned into a parking spot, and I could see him proudly sporting a freshly cut Mohawk. The sunlight caught the diamond in his left ear and it sparkled as he maneuvered the curve in the parking lot. I guess that's what they call *swag*. It all just seemed so appropriate. My son was no longer a boy. He was now a man, making his own decisions about how he would chose to portray and express himself.

I sat on the bench watching all three college quarterbacks that Coach had invited to this session, each at slightly different levels of maturity and development. After about 10 minutes of warm-ups, Coach called the group together and began the class.

"This is the final class. This is the final assessment before we send you off to your respective schools and situations and opportunities, and we sit back and watch the stories of your careers unfold, starting this fall. Let's get some good work done today. Some review, some tune-up, and some reinforcement of the things we have been working on all along. OK? Let's get to work."

The on-field session moved crisply from drill to drill, and the quarterbacks took turns throwing to targets simulating various routes, including slants, seams, quick posts, deep comebacks, corners, and on-the-run throws. All three quarterbacks looked excellent, Shawn as good as I had ever seen. It was easy to see that Coach Wilson was pleased with all three of his students.

As he usually did, Coach called the group together near the end of the session and said positive and encouraging things to each young man. He turned to Shawn and said, "Boy, I don't know what happened to you over the past month away at college, but you are not as good as you are throwing today!" To an outsider, that comment could be taken as derogatory, even quite discouraging. But to those who have seen Coach's style, they know it isn't those things at all. Shawn was throwing the ball extremely well, with accuracy, velocity, and touch as needed. It is what Coach calls passing the football, not just throwing it. What Coach was really saying was: Wow, you are throwing better than I have ever seen. Shawn was a different athlete than the one who left Durham just a month earlier. He had become a college athlete rather than an elite high school athlete. Big difference. His body was becoming toned and his muscles cut. He wasn't Hercules, and in fact he weighed less than he did when he left, but he was stronger, substantially stronger. This isn't all that unusual, though; it happens to nearly every high school athlete who dedicates himself in the college weight room. All of this showed in Shawn's walk and his posture, and it really showed in his throwing. And Coach pointed out that Shawn still had 25 pounds to gain in that weight room, that those throws would be even stronger once he hit 215 on the scales.

Coach went on. "Now, men, when you head back to campus for summer school and workouts, it's on. The competition gets thicker. But there's one thing I know about my quarterbacks. They aren't afraid of competition. In fact, the higher the level of competition, the better for us because we perform better the bigger the stage and the tougher the fight. But you must realize this, men, as the heat gets turned up—and it will get turned up in the next few weeks—you need to rely on your fundamentals and your technique and your knowledge to stay ahead of the competition. And you have something none of the others have—that's your quarterback notebook and all the classes you have been through with me. We have covered everything, men. Rest assured, and I give you my solemn word, there will not be any circumstance or situation that you will face that we haven't covered.

"And then, let me give you this insight. High-level competitions are not won by miles. More like inches. The better the competition, the closer the finish. And in close competitions, the little things, the inches that you can collect along the way, will add up to you winning the job or not. It is likely a series of little things that will tip the scale of the competition in your—or someone else's—favor.

"So make sure you are doing all the little things. Like clapping for a receiver who just dropped your pass. And instead of yelling at him, you encourage him and pump him up to make the next play. Or greeting the defense as those guys come off the field, and congratulating them on a great series or a turnover. Remember, when you lead as a quarterback, you lead not only yourself, but the entire offense. And not only the offense, but the entire team. And not only the team, but the university."

After Coach had gone through the quarterbacks, he thanked the parents who were there and the receivers who had come out to catch balls in this heat. He shook every man's hand, one by one, picked up his cones and notepad, and shuffled off the field toward his car.

The final class for this season of life was over. The students all got their grades, which were passing ones, and with flying colors. It was graduation day. The students were all encouraged, but also challenged, and drove away into their future.

* * * * *

As I walked to my car on the other side of the lot, Coach was standing at his car with his trunk open. Without looking at me, as he stuffed gear in the back compartment, Coach began talking. "Well, Dad, you did a great job. He is ready. As ready as I had hoped, maybe even better than I expected. What I saw today from him was special stuff. His ball was different, his pace and his manner were different. He is a college player now. Shawn told me that the other quarterbacks can really spin the ball, throw it really hard. But I want you to tell him this: it's not about them, it's about Shawn. It's not about the competition; it's about the composition. He can make all the throws to every part of the field. And he is a passer, with touch and timing and anticipation. If he doesn't get hurt, the sky is his limit. I told him that his best defense in the quarterback competition is to keep the ball when they give it to him. Doesn't matter how hard anybody throws if they are on the sidelines watching you."

Coach continued talking, but now he turned to look me in the eye.

"Dad, I am proud of you. From our first chat at Champs restaurant with Shawn's mom 18 months ago, you have done everything you could to be a great father and supportive coach to your son. Through the divorce issues and the visitations and the injury and rehab and the season and the playoffs and recruiting anxiety and then your own leukemia, you have been a rock and a tremendous example of how to be a loving father no matter what. I am proud of you. And you should be proud of yourself."

Fact of the matter is, I was proud of our process and the outcome. And I was a little choked up as well. I just hugged Coach and said, "Thanks, man. We couldn't have done it without you."

FIFTEEN

A Divine Appointment

"We wouldn't have chosen this path, but if we wanted to tell a story, this is the one we would write"

August

With Shawn gone back to finish summer school, and no more classes in the basement or on the turf, no more film to watch, or high school practices to attend, I was lost for a while. This had been a big part of my weekly activities for the last year and a half.

I decided I would put all the notes I had taken and typed from all the classes into one document. So I did, and then took them to the copy center to print. The next day, when I returned, the man handed me a document with more than 300 double-sided pages that he had bound together. "Are you writing a manuscript or something?" he asked. I had never thought of it that way; I had intended to merely print all of this out as a gift for Coach Wilson so he would have a record of all we had gone over and all the stories he had told.

I took the "book" home and started to leaf through it, and I was enthralled. I couldn't put it down, flipping page to page and story to story. I called Coach to set up a meeting to give him a copy, but he wasn't home, and he suggested I just leave it on his

SCOTT STANKAVAGE

doorstep, which I did.

The next week, I got a call from Coach. "Hey, Scott. Coach Wilson here. I was reading through the notes of all our classes that we had with Shawn and began thinking about all the stuff as it has unfolded. I was wondering if you could stop by and come inside with me for a few minutes. There are a couple of things I want to run by you."

I was on my way to an acupuncture appointment, but said I would stop by afterward, in about an hour.

I wondered what Coach wanted to talk about. To tell the truth, he had never asked me into his home before. I didn't find it strange, but I was curious. We usually met for class in my basement, and sometimes we would be at an athletic field or get a bite to eat at a burger joint.

I think Coach realized I had never been in his home, so he came outside to greet me when I pulled into the drive. We walked inside and things were just as I expected: well kept, everything in its place. I always enjoy seeing where a man does his work, looking at his office setup and the pictures around his room. I like to envision the environment he sits in when I am talking to him on the phone. And conversely, I like when the other person has seen and is familiar with my desk and business chair. It's a unique sort of connection that makes conversation and collaboration somehow more enjoyable. So I was honored to be in Coach's home.

He invited me into his office. It is a small room with three computers, six hard drives, and two computer screens all set up. This is where Coach does all his Powerpoints and creates his teaching tools and videos for the Ultimate Football University website. A novice computer person would not know where to start in his command seat. I was actually a little intimidated, seeing where he played his EA Sports Madden games. I knew he had played Shawn remotely from this office. I had been a personal witness to two butt-whippings that Coach put on Shawn while playing Madden during our class time together, and I knew there were more.

Coach turned to me and said, "See those?" He pointed to two

four-foot-tall, thin, Infinity-brand speakers. "Bought those in 1987 in Denver with my Super Bowl money. I told the guy I want them to last the rest of my life. Now this room is too small for all that power, but when I turn them on, along with the other six speakers and the woofer over there, I sit here in my leather chair and just let the music flow through me. I like the strings, that's my kind of music, and sometimes when my head hurts or I am just tangled up in my mind, I come in here and just soak. It's beautiful, man. Every man needs his place of solitude, and this is where I come." I was smiling and even gave him a high five; it was his special place and I was honored Coach was sharing it with me.

But I was also waiting for Coach to set the real agenda.

So he began. "Scott, I have been reading through the book of all the classes you dropped off. And so I am lying in bed the last couple of nights thinking about all the stuff as it has unfolded the last year and half since we came together, and I began to connect the dots. So many times in life we get so absorbed in what is happening in front of us that we miss the bigger picture of what is happening around us. You and I have been connected since that first day in Broncos training camp back in 1984. And thirty years later, we are together again. It is like we have had a divine appointment. And while a lot has changed, some things haven't. Here we are. You and me. Facing some challenges, but we are committed to finding a way through, finding a way to pursue and accomplish our dreams. Back then it was the NFL. Today it is much bigger and more important than that because it involves so many other people. It revolves around our life's work having value beyond our lifetimes and perhaps for generations to come.

"It wasn't just happenstance that we ended up here, Scott. I was in Durham because I was retired. I had been collecting and documenting my entire life's library of football knowledge so that it wouldn't leave this earth when I did. That is why I started Ultimate Football University.

"Then we ran across each other because of your son and the challenges he faced in his career overcoming an ACL and missing the recruiting cycle of evaluation to get all those stars and rankings. He fell off the radar for most colleges.

"And you and his mom came to me and asked me, 'What do we do? How do we get Shawn rated and in the mix for college scholarships?' The truth was, I didn't exactly know.

"But do you realize that is what thousands of parents ask themselves every year around the country, and spend hundreds of thousands of dollars pursuing—something they don't even know, well, exactly what it is?

"So we went ahead and created our own quarterback school. Instead of getting what we wanted, we got what we needed.

"Dad"—Coach often had this endearing way of calling me Dad—"a year ago you would have been dancing in the streets if your son had been selected to the Elite 11 quarterback combine on ESPN. But here is the deal: that show is a made-for-TV reality series. And we see now that would not have been the best thing to happen to Shawn. Because he would not have been sitting in our class with a chip on his shoulder and carrying an urgency that kept him focused on getting better every day regardless of what others said about him.

"The very things that look like they were setbacks were actually setups. Setups for success."

Coach had plenty to say, and kept going. "What I taught Shawn about the game is exactly what I taught my college quarterbacks all those years so they would learn to not need me during a game, but rather would be able to find the answer for themselves in the middle of the play on the field. That is how we developed so many NFL-caliber players from such a small school. It was out of necessity. I ended up teaching our quarterbacks to be coaches on the field in the action, not puppets reading posters with pictures of cars and ducks and ice cream cones being flashed from the sidelines before every play. No! Our quarterbacks could think for themselves and lead their team because they were equipped, authorized, and empowered to make decisions in split-seconds on how to protect themselves and how to defeat the defense. That is the beauty and the joy of our stack learning.

"We talked about it often. It is not just the pure knowledge that we are after. It is the knowing of the information so that we can spontaneously convert the knowledge we have into on-field execution. I want our players to be able to do what they think. And that means on both fronts, mentally and physically. They have to be able to process what they see and then be able to mechanically execute what they intend. It's all connected. And we know it works. We teach our quarterbacks all they need for success: the mechanics, the knowledge, and how to process it all in a split-second.

"So, we went into your basement, Scott, and we began to lay out what Shawn needed to be successful in his high school senior season. But we didn't limit our goal to just that. We expanded it to teach him what he would need to play in college and in the SEC. And we even were so bold as to suggest what he was learning was the same stuff he would need one day if he ever had a chance to play in the NFL. And we followed the NFL draft combines and saw so many top college quarterbacks get criticized for not having this information available to them in their films with Gruden [TV analyst Jon] and in their mechanics analyzed by Kurt Warner [former Rams and Cardinals Super Bowl quarterback] at the combines. It is obvious; we were 100 percent on the right track and possibly even ahead of the curve in quarterback teaching.

"But think about this. We came together because we were responding to being snubbed and left out by the existing system of the recruiting, marketing, and coaching of quarterbacks."

Coach was winding to a conclusion, but he had still more.

"I learned offense for the purpose of playing defense. And then I learned defense from the perspective of playing offense. Joe Collier, my defensive coordinator at the Broncos, was notorious for making us learn the weakness of each defense so we could protect it. And he did that by making us learn offense and making us understand how the offense would attack our defense. That is why I am certain that we must teach all parts of the game to the quarterback, so he can be empowered physically and mentally to always know how to attack. There are thousands of parents every year, every single year out there, who would give almost anything to get this information and give this class to their sons.

"But instead, young quarterback prospects chase the 5-star rating system. And let me be clear, the ranking system isn't broken. What it *is* is commercial. The ESPN and Rivals and Nike and 247Sports websites all are focused on driving Internet traffic to their websites and then being able to sign up advertisers who want to access the audience they have captured. Fact is that, often the guys giving the ratings are journalists, not coaches! The ratings are based on who has the most colleges interested in these players. And the combines invite the most hyped athletes so they can get the most media coverage, which means more website hits and more viewers on ESPN.

"Unfortunately, the hype eventually has very little to do with the future careers these young men will have. In fact, if you look at the last ten years of the Elite 11 quarterback participants, less than half of them ever start as a quarterback in college. You find yourself asking: *What? That can't be right.* How can the best of the best as judged by the current ranking system have such an incredibly low success rate in translating high school prospects into college quarterbacks?

"I will tell you part of the reason why. Because these kids get so hyped and expectations get so high that they can actually be doomed by the weight of their own potential and its expectations. When they get to college, and players, coaches, and the media figure out that they are not as fully developed as the hype suggests, the fall from grace can be a long way down. And they are only 18 years old, totally unprepared to be so whiplashed from first the praise from adoring fans and media one year and then totally taken out with the trash the next season! It's a tough road, the system in place, how these young men are treated. It's not their fault. But in the end, they are the ones who suffer. And nobody tells them or their families what to really expect. They get a shot, they fail, and they are passed over for another guy. Over 25 percent of Elite 11 quarterback finalists transfer from their first college. It's not that they don't have potential. But it must be developed and coached—continually.

"Here's the thing. The combines and rankings are based on what people call 'arm talent' or how far and hard a kid can throw the ball against air or in some basic 7-on-7 passing scrimmages. And that is all good, but it is my strong belief that being a scientist of the game is more valuable than arm talent. And a scientist with arm talent is a Hall of Famer: see Aaron Rodgers, Tom Brady, and Drew Brees. But arm talent alone won't win the day. It's not enough.

"So, looking back, in one sense, the best thing that could have happened to Shawn was his ACL, which forced him to give up basketball, prioritize football, and commit to becoming the best quarterback he could imagine both physically and mentally. And that is what we did.

"And now he got into his dream school, the one he told us in his junior season he wanted to attend, Vanderbilt University in the SEC."

Coach leaned back and took a deep breath.

"Let me wrap this up for you, Scott. The urgency your son had to face from his ACL injury and then the urgency you faced with your leukemia both created the basis for our classes together. And you have spent the last 18 months documenting all of the football that I have collected over 35 years. This package is valuable to almost every coach and every quarterback in America. It can teach them about football, and the process, and about recruiting, and about the perception versus the reality. And it can teach them about life, and it can be used for their entire lives. The message to all quarterbacks everywhere is this: 'Don't be bitter if you aren't in the hype machine.' And if you are, enjoy the smoke, but realize that where there is smoke there is fire, and fire means you can get burned. So, make no mistake, the hype is *not* necessary for your success and has very little to do with the ultimate outcome. The hype is for frills, so whether you are hyped or not, don't lose focus on the work that needs to get done.

"I've spent my life as a coach trying to find and bring hope to situations that seemed hopeless. And as I sat back last night thinking about it all, I realized that this can be my greatest effort and offering. And I want it to be part of my legacy. To know that my life's work has value, lasting value, that I was able to share it with others for their benefit, enjoyment, and empowerment.

"Last night, I tried to recount my mentors and what I retained from each of them. I smiled as I thought about coach Doug Parker, the Hall of Famer who recruited me to Howard University. That's who I get my storytelling from, because he started off every meeting with a story of some kind. Man, talk about a guy who could paint a picture and inspire and encourage a team: it was him. Then there was coach Tom Landry, the icon, on the Mount Rushmore of coaching. He impressed on me the power of every detail, of knowing everybody's assignment on every play. He wasn't very personable with his players because he didn't want it to cloud his judgment when he had to make cuts, but he was fair.

"And then there was Dan Reeves, who was a player-coach for the Cowboys. He was a fiery competitor and just like Coach Landry in a lot of ways, but he was more personable and approachable for his players. And then, lastly, when I think of my mentors, there is my dad. I learned a lot from him, but the thing that he really impressed upon me was his reverence for the quarterback of a football team. He played with four Hall of Fame quarterbacks—Van Brocklin, Waterfield, Unitas, Tarkenton—and was coached by another, Sid Gillman. And then I played with Staubach and Elway, and I learned to have the same respect and admiration for those men, who were gifted enough to be championship quarterbacks. And my dad was the first one to really teach me this.

"And that is part of the reason I have an affinity for training quarterbacks, because I have been exposed to the best of the best. And I know what they look like and act like and how they lead. And I believe there are elements of greatness that can be taught and learned.

"Because you know, for a kid like Shawn, talent is not enough.

And for other kids, information is not enough. But when talent and information come together, greatness is available.

"And we all know this from our own life experience: *Everybody* gets a chance somewhere in time to show what they can do. We need to keep telling Shawn not to worry about when that is. Whether it's the first game or the third or next spring or next fall. It will come. But make him promise to keep his head in that book of class material we've compiled. It's all there for him. It's not 'an edge'—it's the answer!"

I realized that this was Coach Steve Wilson connecting the dots of his lifetime and looking around at what exists and what doesn't exist and realizing that what we have created has value to many people for many reasons.

And suddenly I realized our story—this story of *The QB Mentor*—wasn't exclusively for just my son and me. It could help lots of young men and their families—on and off the football field.

Epilogue:
The Class Continues

*"In some ways, it's just another chapter that will make it
even more incredible when it all plays out"*

For Shawn's freshman year at Vanderbilt, the decision was
made to place him on redshirt status. For those not familiar,
that's a common term that means a player does not use a year
of eligibility (so four full years of athletic play remain), but he
cannot compete in games.

Vanderbilt went 3-9 during that first fall. Shawn felt, and we
all felt, that the quarterback classes he had gone through with
Coach brought him added respect on the scout field and in various
meetings. Shawn then moved forward toward 2015 and the
Vanderbilt spring game.

* * * * *

I had the good fortune of introducing Coach Wilson at a football
coaches' clinic at Howard University last spring. It was quite
a privilege for me as I shared that I would be writing this book
to honor Coach for the impact he has had on my family the past
two years.

I got to meet many of his former Howard players, who had
come back to hear him speak, along with a panel of his past
players now coaching in the pros or college, including Jimmy
Johnson, Pep Hamilton, Roy Anderson, Gary Harrell, and Ted
White. Over the course of two days I had dozens of men come
up to me and tell me how influential Coach had been on their
lives—not just in their football careers, but their business careers

and their marriages. We traded stories and laughed at the anecdotes that Coach used 20 years ago that he is still using today. They apply today because they are still just as impactful and true.

* * * * *

For Coach, there is also the reality of having played ten long years in the National Football League. It isn't a "physical" or "tough" sport. It is a violent sport. The men are indeed gladiators. Coach lived this life for ten years.

I remember one meeting we had at the mall. As we left, I was driving through the parking lot when I noticed Coach in the middle of the lot, looking lost. I pulled up to him and he said, sheepishly, "Funny, I don't remember where I parked my car." So he got into my car and we drove around until we found it. Coach said that sometimes this happens, but he doesn't think much of it.

There were times I would worry a bit about Coach. I remember some of our basement sessions with the whiteboard. There were a few times when Coach would lose his train of thought. I once asked him about it. Coach replied that he had basically stopped doing public speaking because he didn't like to lose his train of thought in front of others.

After one class, Coach called me the next morning and asked, "Hey, did I leave my mouse in the basement last night?" He had, and invariably that would happen. I would run the mouse over to his place so he could get his work done.

* * * * *

Regarding my health, as of the final work on this book, in fall 2015, I was enjoying an extended, surprising, and welcomed second remission from the special type of leukemia that I face. The doctors admit to being pleasantly surprised, although I know all the prayer is working, in addition to the state-of-the-art research and science at Duke Medical Center and around the world. Truth is, these are not impossible odds at this stage of my life. I battle on. All the things I learned in our classes have given me added resolve.

Once when we were discussing the book, Coach stopped and said, "Did I ever tell you about the time I stepped on the eight ball in my son's room, and what an omen that was for our team?"

In fact he had. He had previously told me how, in 1996, his Howard University team opened the season 1-2 and, to rub salt in the wound, was stranded at a Florida airport after losing a game to Florida A&M; the team charter had forgot to come and pick the team up following the game! But I didn't let on with Coach that I had heard it, as hearing the story again, like most of coach's recounts, might reveal another insight that I had missed the first time. So I just answered, "No, go ahead."

So Coach set the scene again, telling how he walked into his son's room late at night when he finally got home and, in the dark, stepped on one of the boy's toys. It was a miniature pool ball, the black eight ball. He took it as an omen, and the next day he gave a speech to the team using that eight ball, and said that he knew what they had to do. "We are going to run the table. We are going to go 8-0 the rest of the season." And that's exactly what Howard did. Led by Ted White, its All-American quarterback, Howard ended up winning a New Year's Eve bowl game, the Heritage Bowl, that year as well.

Coach paused, then looked at me and said, "That's what you are doing, Scott, with this leukemia, with Kate and your littlest kids, marrying your oldest daughters, and fathering Shawn. Man, you are running the table. I am proud of you. Keep it up!"

I couldn't have been more inspired. That's just what Coach does.

Here is a postscript on my battle: my faith has proven strong and enduring. Although I do think about and am faced with the reality of my leukemia every day, I no longer think (as I used to, and every day) about when I might die. I don't think that each holiday or each family gathering could be my last . . . my faith and my family have grown past that worry, those fears, and the reality is that it is not a fear for me any longer. I have a peace about the future, whether it is Shawn's career or my daughters' marriages or my leukemia—we are all in good hands.

I am trusting the power of prayer, and medicine, and the doctors and researchers who tell me that science is within three to five years of curing blood cancers. I am reassured and able to focus on the one thing that matters most: my family.

* * * * *

Back at Vanderbilt, Shawn didn't get all the reps he would have liked in his first spring practice in his bid to become the starting quarterback, and truthfully, he was pretty disappointed. Coach said to me, "That's exactly what we want to hear from him: that it matters, that it hurts, that it pisses him off, and that he has to figure out how to change the situation."

I went to the spring game not expecting Shawn to get any snaps, and preparing to encourage him to continue to work and study and make himself better.

But he did get in, and Shawn looked comfortable and relaxed on the field. It was exciting to see him playing football again, and I realized how much joy it brought me simply watching him play.

Shawn ended up 8 for 11 for 67 yards and no turnovers in that spring game. He had been the most efficient Commodore quarterback by far; he led the only scoring drive in all offensive possessions. I was so proud of him and his performance, especially given the fact that he didn't even expect to play.

The game had been televised by the SEC Network, and the announcers had plenty of positive things to say about Shawn, including, "He is a smart, heady player who manages the pocket well, keeps his eyes downfield, and when he escapes, he looks to pass first. He doesn't panic and presses into the pocket nicely. He manages the passing game well."

I don't think I could have written a script any better to describe one of Coach Wilson's quarterback pupils.

* * * * *

When I got back home to North Carolina, Shawn called me in the middle of the week after the spring game. He reported great meetings with his quarterback coach and head coach Mason. "They want me to get ready to play next season, Dad. They want me to get bigger and stronger, so I will be staying here through the summer so I can lift and work out with the guys."

I just sat there with a deep smile. Eventually, I asked him, "How are you feeling about where you are?"

And then everything took a turn, a turn I never would have expected. Shawn said he felt great, but told me he had ice on his left knee—the reconstructed one—because it was swollen.

When I asked what happened, he said, "I don't know. In this morning's workout I kind of tweaked it and I told the strength coach and he took me out of the squat exercise. But I finished the workout and just iced it for my meeting with Coach Mason."

* * * * *

Late the next morning my cell buzzed. It was Shawn. I quickly answered.

The next words from Shawn were like getting hit in the face with a two-by-four. "Dad, not good. They did an MRI last night and it shows I re-tore my ACL." Shawn's voice trailed off into tears.

I burst into tears myself. It felt like some kind of emotional combustion. I moved the phone away from my face so Shawn would not hear my sobs. I took a minute to compose myself.

"Hey son, that just sucks. That ticks me off for you. I am so mad." I was still trying to gain my composure. The thing I *didn't* want to do was to break into some fake-sounding, false lyric about how this happened for a reason and that it was all part of a wonderful, larger plan. I didn't want to minimize the gravity and devastation of this news. It was horrible, and I wanted Shawn to know he was not alone in being devastated.

"I can't believe it, Dad. Just as I thought I was going to get my chance," Shawn said through tears.

I gathered my thoughts as quickly as I could. "Hey, let's realize one thing, and that is that the Lord hasn't abandoned you. He brought you here and he has a plan to get you out of here. I know that for certain." Our conversation continued, but I'll keep the rest between my son and myself for now.

Truth is, I was devastated. I was helpless, again. There was nothing I could do to change Shawn's injury or his pain.

* * * * *

I called Coach Wilson that evening.

He was devastated.

"You know I love him like he is my own son," Coach said. There was silence. I think even Coach got choked up on the other end of the phone.

I told Coach how mad I was at the entire situation. He empathized, but then went quickly on to add: "But here is the thing to realize: before you or Shawn or your family move into making the plan to overcome this moment, you first have to let yourself experience the grief of the moment. This is heavy, man, and it's gonna take some time to feel bad and let it sink in.

"But the reality is also this: after we get through the grief, this story will have just gotten even better. It gives him more time to prepare and to get bigger and stronger and ready himself for when he does play. It's interesting, isn't it? The timing of these events? The affirmation he received from the coaches and his teammates and the media, and then the injury. He showed everyone who he is and who he can be for them. He gave them hope. The story doesn't end here. No. In some ways, it's just another chapter that will make it even more incredible when it all plays out."

This is Coach, always the optimist, always looking past what has happened to what we will do, together, to respond.

* * * * *

As of early fall 2015, Shawn was feeling fantastic, his rehab once again ahead of schedule. He was already throwing and running passing drills with teammates just four months after surgery, as well as jogging.

Coach told Shawn about one of his favorite players that he coached, Marcus Douglas. He was a defensive lineman who overcame two ACL tears to have a 12-year NFL career with the Baltimore Ravens, New York Jets, and San Francisco 49ers. Coach told Shawn, "A great career after two knee surgeries is not impossible. It just takes a little more work, that's all."

Coach had more that he shared with Shawn in that summer after the second ACL knee tear.

"You see, if you are gonna do something big in life, Shawn, you have to see it first, and then you have to *say it*. You have to profess it with your lips, because you don't really put yourself out there until you say it out loud in front of others. Doing that gives you something to play for; it makes you find a way even in the darkest of moments, because there is no way out except to get it done. It puts a silent pressure on yourself that enables you to access places and strengths and faith and performance that you otherwise can't get to.

"The way I see it, this second ACL injury is exactly that. Life creates resolve. It is not created on its own through ordinary everyday circumstance. You can get it late, or early, or right on time, but without it, you will not meet your ultimate destiny."

* * * * *

For Coach Wilson, new versions of his class go on with coaches and high school and college quarterbacks. We like to say that he has "new kids in the chamber" as he dispenses his rare breed of wisdom. His mentoring continues.

And so our collective journey winds on, and we don't know where it will take Shawn. Or myself. Or Coach.

Looking back on all the classes that we had together, I think it was ultimately about empowerment. Coach said during one session that "empowerment at its very basic level is to hold on to the vision for someone's life long enough until they can see the vision for themselves."

In many ways, that is what the quarterback classes did for all of us.

They kept alive my vision to be healthy enough to see my son play out his high school career. And they keep me motivated today to change my diet and exercise and take the medicines and the alternative energy and healing work that is outside of my normal routine so I can be there if Shawn gets to play in college. But at even deeper levels, I keep this vision: to walk my two youngest daughters down the aisle, and even to hear the laughter of my children's children, to one day hold my very own grandbaby.

Whether my remission continues, or Shawn ever plays quarterback in college, or if Coach ever mentors another quarterback or coach, our time together can't ever be taken away. It has truly been an incredible journey. I am honored to tell just a part of Coach Wilson's story, the part interwoven between Coach, Shawn, and me.

Wisdom from Coach

Some of Coach Steve Wilson's best lessons, pulled together in one place.

LIFE AND LEADERSHIP

The Journey

A secret of life is that the most joy is found in the moments during the journey, not in the moment of arrival at the destination. Unfortunately, nobody tells you this along the way.

The guys on top of the mountain didn't just fall there.

To beat competition you will never know or see, you must do all you can do, and then do a little bit more.

Control

You must control what you pursue; you must not let it control you. You control the quality of your work, always.

Control the controllables! Don't worry about the other stuff.

Control your perception, or it will control you.

Attitude

Everybody has 24 hours in a day. There are no exceptions. It's what you do with your 24 hours that matters when in competition. The guy who gives up more of his 24 hours [sacrifices self, and personal time] usually wins.

Do what you have to do so that you can do what you want to do.

You have to do what you have never done to get what you have never had.

The most important lesson I will ever teach you is this: that you realize that whatever you need, you can find it in your body. Whether it is speed or acceleration or power or torque or information, you can find it in yourself. But we have to put it there first.

If you aren't chasing something, then you are not in competition.

The toughest skins come from the toughest animals. You have to take criticism and coaching and allow it to make you better and fuel your fire. Coaches always want to know how a player responds to adversity.

It's OK to be your own worst critic at times. But you better also be your own biggest fan far more often.

The most important voice to hear in your head is your own. You always have the last word!

Many people use a "bad attitude" as an excuse to underachieve. Attitude is not a condition of your environment. Attitude is not connected to your financial status. Attitude is not a medical condition with no known cure. Every day you must wake up and realize that *your attitude is a decision* you must make about your *outlook to compete or take a seat.*

Mental Approach, Discipline

Being selfish with your dreams also means being selfish with your time.

Learning is like using chopsticks: it's one thing to read about using them, another to actually use them, and another to become skilled at using them.

You must know the moves of each chess piece before you enter a master chess competition!

People either create problems or solve them. Be a problem-solver.

To become great at anything, you must pursue *mastery*.

Pressure explodes pipes, but it also makes diamonds.

Every day you must find your own motivation! Don't wait for somebody to jump-start you. You must be excited about finding something that drives you toward your goals. Going through the motions will not lead to greatness. Learn to compete in *everything*, and if you defeat all competitors around you, then learn to compete with yourself. Ultimately, that is the greatest game of all, competing with yourself to become the best you can possibly be!

Effort

Why worry about being the underdog? Why worry about not having the resources of other people? Why worry about your lack of opportunity? Why worry about the uncertainty in your life? The Great Equalizer in life is time, and we all have the same 24 hours in a day. What separates you is your effort. You see, effort is *free*. Every day, do all that you can do, and then a little bit more. If an opportunity comes to you, you will be ready. *When* opportunity comes to you is none of your business.

Faith

Faith isn't faith until it's all you are left holding onto.

Educated faith is a powerful force in this life.

Faith in something gets stronger the more you use it. The more you can see it, the sooner you can *be it*. Your vision of what you want will take you to what you want. Remember, believing in something first requires initiative, and that is a characteristic that losers just don't have.

Faith is a muscle and, like any muscle, the more you use it the bigger and stronger it becomes.

Preparation

It's not how strong you are physically, it's how strong your mind and body are together *as one*!

The question is: how quick will you pursue mastery? How many reps does it take you to pick up a technique?

For a quarterback, *doubt* is the same as *not knowing*.

Fight sloppiness at all times.

Separation through preparation!

Preparation takes place in the dark, away from the spotlight.

I guarantee you: Tuesday's notes *always* show up in the game on Saturday! In life, always do your homework *before* it is required.

Excellence, Success, Greatness

Greatness has two components: One, the pursuit of perfection. Two: *despise* sloppiness.

Men follow men who can do things that they can't!

People make people, not stadiums or weight rooms or buildings.

You get what you tolerate.

Don't focus on the pain or difficulty of the mission. Focus on what you want and *eat the pain!*

Athletic greatness is the ability to, on command, have your brain ask your body do something it has never done before. Then, in the moment of competition, your body delivers.

We live in a world of fast-changing technology, and there are two things needed to be successful: money and information. You can get money from almost anyplace and it can disappear quickly. Information is acquired mostly through research and education, and it lasts forever. At the end of the day, if you have money, for a price you can buy information. On the other hand, if you have information you can always make money.

This is what I call "when as in win!" . . . When exhausting things are easy. When demanding things are painless. When difficult things can be done immediately, and when impossible things only take time. *Then* you have separated yourself from everyone else, and you will be ready when your opportunity arrives . . . and you will win!

Greatness is illustrated when you can make the play when you absolutely have to have it, and that usually isn't until the fourth quarter!

Perspective

Sometimes obscurity in life is a blessing. Use it wisely.

You become great in the darkness, in the desert, not in the spotlight.

You must eventually beat an opponent that you may never see.

The most important part of your life is the dash. [See chapter 9.]

Some caterpillars come out of the cocoon later than others.

Don't get too worked up over how others view how you work, how you live, or how you play. Do what you think is needed to be successful and don't worry about the many courts of opinion.

The giraffe and the turtle share the same watering hole and breathe the same air and walk through the same grass, but they will never have the same perspective on life. It is that way with humans as well.

What you say to yourself is ten times more important than what others say to you or about you. Make sure you are saying the things you *need* to hear, and not what you *want* to hear.

Friends and Companions; Types of People

As a person you are a product of the people in your life and your experiences. If the people that surround you are great in one way or another, you won't have to worry about the quality of your experiences. Keep in mind my definition of a great person: someone who does something for another and looks for nothing in return.

Life has these types of people:
- Those who are on the way and those who are in the way.
- Those who are committed and those who are involved.
- Those who push the wagon and those who ride in the wagon.
- Those who dream and those who sleep.
- Those who listen and those who complain.
- Those who create solutions and those who create problems.

. . . If you know people who are the latter case in each one of these statements, as quick as you can, move as far away from them as possible.

Don'ts

- Don't let complacency become you.
- Don't let fear persuade you.
- Don't let failure frustrate you.
- Don't let success change you!

ON FOOTBALL

Love of the Game

There is only one game of football. Learn it and you can play it at any level. Learn it and you can apply it and love it for the rest of your life.

You must talk football to yourself. All the time.

In order to change somebody's mind, you must do it with what they see, not what you say.

Certainly there are risks involved in playing the game of football. There is also a risk in living without the lessons that the game teaches us.

I watch your hips, not your lips.

Quarterbacking

Quarterbacking is a lifestyle, and it's non-negotiable.

Quarterbacks must seek mastery in three areas: mechanics, knowledge, and mental processing.

Knowledge is not power; it is *potential* power. Execution is mastery, and execution trumps knowledge every time.

The goal is to turn knowledge into manipulation, and to compress response into reaction.

It's not about the competition; it's about your composition.

Speculate . . . confirm . . . compute . . . execute!

Quarterbacks must work in a state of contingency all the time, always ready for the worst case, with no time and no space, but still able to execute for their team.

The quarterback life: He cannot be who he wants to be. He must be who he has to be. During adverse times the most important thing is *perception*, and it will not be how he feels about himself, it will only be how everyone else feels about him.

A quarterback's first job description is to *win*. How much he wins is greatly affected by how he leads. How he leads is determined by how he lives. How he lives is mostly about how much he gives.

Imagination
A great passer must throw into a future that is not there yet . . . . at the intersection of time and speed and the arc of the ball and the break of the receiver . . . it all comes together in the exact moment of perfect execution.

Execution and the Pursuit of Perfection
When San Francisco 49ers Head Coach Bill Walsh told quarterback Joe Montana to "hit the receiver in the eye," Joe asked: "Which eye?"

You control the quality of your work. Never put sloppy work on tape. Take pride in every rep.

Focus *more* when you are tired; use fatigue to sharpen your skills over your competition.

Remember, it's not unsound if you don't expose it and exploit it.

Physical

You can't play fast if your feet go slow.

If you think slow and your feet move slow, you are a slug, not a quarterback.

On Beating the Defense

Remember, a defender's alignment—even if it's excellent—is not his *technique*. There is no disguise after the snap: a man must get to his work, or he gets beat.

Every player on every play has a run and a pass responsibility. Know what they are and exploit his conflict.

How can you win a chess match if you don't know what all the pieces can do? Same in a football game on offense. Learn every defensive rule and adjustment.

Handling the Blitz

Be ready for the gorilla loose in the kitchen.

A quarterback must participate in his own protection!

A successful blitz just brings more blitz. The only anecdote is to burn the blitz . . . and then they will back off.

They can only come from where they are.

Always set your protection to your blind side; you want to see a robber if he is in your kitchen with a baseball bat trying to hit you in the head. Never get hit in the back of the head as a quarterback!

The quarterback determines who will come unblocked.

Never throw hot if you can avoid it. Always try and pick up the blitzers with protection.

The Classmates

Coach Steve Wilson, former NFL player and college head coach

The son of former NFL half-back Tom Wilson—nicknamed "Touchdown Tommy" because of his prolific scoring ability—Steve Wilson grew up with football running through his veins. It was no surprise, then, that he was an all-state player in high school and a standout wide receiver at Howard University before moving on to play the same position with the Dallas Cowboys  in 1979. Steve left Dallas after three seasons, joining the Denver Broncos in 1982. He played cornerback for his seven seasons in Denver, where he excelled and ultimately started at cornerback in two Super Bowls.

Steve's ability to play both sides of the ball and learn all positions gave him a unique advantage when he began his head coaching career at his alma mater, Howard, in 1989. He stayed at Howard until 2001 and then moved on to the positions of defensive coordinator at Bowie State and head coach at Texas Southern, all while racking up accolades that included MEAC Conference Coach of the Year (1989 and 1993), Division I-AA Most Improved Team in 1992, MEAC Conference Champion in 1993 (with an 11-0 record), and a 2003 Bowie State team whose defense so dominated opposing offenses that it set numerous records. During the 1990s Wilson's team winning percentage was 70 percent, and his team was named Black College national champions twice. His 1993 team competed in the NCAA Division I-AA (now FCS) playoffs for the first time in school history. He is

Howard's winningest football coach and his Howard Bisons won the Heritage Bowl in 1996.

Several of his players earned All-Conference honors, All-American accolades, and Player of the Year recognition. Wilson's former players include Roy Anderson (Indianapolis Colts), Pep Hamilton (offensive coordinator, Stanford, followed by holding the same position with the Indianapolis Colts), Gary Harrell (Howard University head coach), Jay Walker (ESPN analyst and former I-AA national Player of the Year), Ted White (offensive coordinator at Howard), and Jimmy Johnson (coach with the New York Jets). Several played professionally in the NFL.

Wilson is a member of the Black College Hall of Fame and was named a MEAC Challenge Legend in 2012.

To contact Coach Steve Wilson, write to ufu45@yahoo.com.

Scott Stankavage, former NFL quarterback

Scott Stankavage is a former high school All-American quarterback/defensive back who finished a notable career at the University of North Carolina with seven passing records and a 16-5 record as a starter. Following graduation (Scott earned a B.S. in business administration in 1984), he signed with the Denver Broncos as a free agent. From 1984 to 1986, he was a member of teams that included John Elway, linebacker Tom Jackson (now ESPN analyst), and Gary Kubiak, and was coached by NFL greats Dan Reeves and Mike Shanahan. He finished his NFL career with the 1987 Miami Dolphins, playing for coach Don Shula.

After football, Scott turned his attention to real estate, where he began a 30-year career as a commercial real estate broker in the Raleigh/Durham, North Carolina area. He specializes in large commercial leases and sale transactions. Scott has strong philanthropic interests that include serving as a board member of the Durham Eagles Pop Warner football organization and including funding $1,000 college scholarships for any boy participating for five years in the program. He started the Turning Point Adolescent Center, a mental health care agency for families in the Durham area. Scott is a past board member for the Bishops Annual Appeal in the Catholic Diocese of Raleigh and the Durham YMCA. He is a volunteer at the Ronald McDonald House in Chapel Hill and attends Chapel Hill Bible Church.

Scott is a married father of seven, his children ranging from 27 to 4.

To contact Scott, visit his website, scottstankavage.com.

Charitable donations can be made directly to the *Scott Stankavage Family Fund* at the Triangle Community Foundation (trianglecf.org) or directly to the Leukemia and Lymphoma Society (LLS).

Shawn Stankavage,
Vanderbilt University quarterback

Shawn is a proud son, big brother, and was an elite high school quarterback at Cardinal Gibbons High School in Raleigh, North Carolina. He also starred in basketball through his sophomore year (he did not play his junior and senior years). He was recruited in football by several universities, choosing Vanderbilt University in Nashville, Tennessee in February 2014.

He overcame a left ACL knee injury tear his junior year in high school to lead his team to the second round of the state playoffs, and a gut-wrenching last-second loss, in his senior season. He redshirted his first year at

Vanderbilt, prepared for play for his first season in fall 2015, and performed well in the Vanderbilt spring game in March 2015, impressing coaches, fans, and media.

Within days of that performance, however, for reasons still not entirely clear, Shawn re-tore his left ACL. Surgery and intense rehab followed once again and Shawn battles to compete for the starting quarterback position at Vanderbilt once his knee recovers. His ultimate athletic goal is to follow his dad's footsteps and play in the National Football League.